Homemade Church

Homemade Church

Written and Illustrated by

Wendy Hamilton

ZealAus Publishing

Homemade Church

Copyright © 2019 by Wendy Hamilton
Illustrations © 2019 by Wendy Hamilton

www.zealauspublishing.com

All rights reserved. No part of this book may be reproduced or transmitted in any form or by any means without written permission of the author. Some names have been changed to protect the identity of persons.

Note this is a rewrite of Wendys previous book "Help! I Hate Church" (Prevoiusly published by AuthorHouse). It has been updated and renamed to better reflect the contents of this book.

ISBN: 978-1-925888-36-2 (e)
ISBN: 978-1-925888-37-9 (hc)
ISBN: 978-1-925888-38-6 (sc)

Dedication

To my Father
who was the thinking
behind much of what we did.

Contents

Unraveling and Re-knitting Church. 1
The Vision 7
The Birth of the Mount Tiger Chapel. 14
Sitting in Hot water 20
The Elephant 26
in the Church 26
The Ways of Animals, children, and Men 30
Chapel Sunday. 35
Fellowship without a Wage Packet. 43
Puffer Fish 52
Hot Air Balloons and the Woman's Voice. 55
Passing on the Baton. 59
The Old Hag or the Young Lady?. 64
Horses and Water Bugs. 69
Sand Flies. 73
The Building Project. 76
Take Off 84
Chrystal 87
Changing Fashions. 93
The Second Child. 96
Father and Son Weekends. 103
Boys and Legs. 112
Mary. 119
Shoemaker Discipleship. 126
The End of the Picnic. 129
About the Author 136
Other Books By Wendy Hamilton 138

Homemade Church

Unraveling and Re-knitting Church.

Matthew 9:16
No man putteth a piece of new cloth unto an old garment for that which is put in to fill it up taketh from the garment, and the rent is made worse. Neither do men put new wine into old bottles: else the bottles break, and the wine runneth out and the bottles perish: but they put new wine into new bottles, and both are preserved.

My mother often unraveled old sweaters and re-knitted them into lovely new garments. When I turned thirteen, she taught me to knit cabled sweaters. For pocket money, I knitted them for the New Zealand tourist industry. I got the impression through knitting these, that the average tourist resembled a gorilla, great big bodies and huge long arms. I did not complain,

Wendy Hamilton

however, as I was paid by the pound. Mum weighed the sweaters on her kitchen scales, the further the kitchen scale hand went around the more elated I grew.

You see, I nursed the dream of most thirteen-year-old girls; I wanted a horse. How many of the wool monsters I knitted to gain the money I needed, I don't recall, but I vividly remember the day I took possession of my eighty-year-old horse. Experts say horses do not live that long, but then they had never seen Wuzzel.

The bay pony had wrinkles and hollows around her eyes. Her bottom lip sagged into a little pouch and one leg did not work too efficiently with the result she walked and cantered but did not trot. She was not beautiful, but I loved her and lavished time and attention on her.

When it became apparent that Wuzzel was lonely and needed a paddock mate, Mum answered an advertisement in the paper and won a free-to-good-home horse.

The free horse was a young sixty. Pretty Lady was a big gentle ex-stock horse. Although she never had a foal, Pretty lady was very maternal and made-do with calves. Motherhood had reduced her thick tail to a strange little fuzz as the calves chewed off most of the hair, much like a toddler loves all the fluff off his teddy bear.

My sister and I had a wonderful time playing with the old geriatrics. We braided their manes and tucked flowers behind their ears, ready for the tea party of carrots and apples we had prepared for them. Once they

Homemade Church

had eaten, their rumps made good slides, and their backs were perfect platforms for climbing trees. Sometimes we packed a picnic lunch and Antoinette and I ambled off for the day, the two of us doubling on Pretty Lady (who had four sturdy legs) and leading Wuzzel (to spare her rickety ones.)

From time to time, we held horse shows. In the days preceding, we made red and blue rosettes out of scrap ribbon and cardboard, laboring over them to make them as realistic as possible. Then in the old quarry, we had our show.

The high side bank made a great grandstand for the judge, (uninterested-in-horses sister number three.) We did not need a judge as the outcome was always the same. (Pretty Lady won the trotting class and Wuzzel won the three-legged race.) We had a judge purely because we wanted to be like the A and P show.

Every year in summer, the big Agricultural and Pastoral Show was held in the local showgrounds. All the farmers from around the district came with their goats, and pigs, and cows, and vegetables, and preserves. The horses, (always the stars of the show) were not owned by the farmers.

"Horse's puh, rough on fences and eat too much," was the typical attitude.

The few that did keep horses used them to work the steep difficult country. No stock horses went to the A and P show. The sleek beauties prancing about belonged to breeders and serious competitors.

Wendy Hamilton

We played tea parties with our ponies

Homemade Church

No pottering around paddocks or horsey tea parties for these ponies or kids. The focus of adults and children alike was winning. In summer they loaded the horses into big trucks and headed off to whatever town was hosting a show that weekend. The days between the shows were devoted to training. They took everything connected to horses very seriously and nursed dreams of the Olympics. We did not even own a saddle, but these families often had more than the value of a house invested in equipment and animals. On show days my sister and I sat on the sidelines in our homely pink sun hats and envied those professional-looking riders on their professional looking horses. It is funny how age changes your perspective; I do not believe they had a fraction of the fun we did with our old nags.

Just as my mother unraveled old sweaters, the western church needs unraveling and re-knitting. Scratch below the surface of Mr. and Mrs. Average Christian and you will find dissatisfaction; burdened women and bored men. From New Zealand to America, pastors and laymen are searching for a makeover. Churches have become like A and P shows where only the best perform, using equipment worth more than most families will ever own. Even the spectators on the sidelines have not escaped the pressure to perform. Bible studies, teaching, seminars and SUPPORTING THE PROGRAM leave little time for fellowship and friendship building. Marriages are breaking up, families are falling apart and nobody has time for the plain old hanging out together and having fun that builds relationships.

We are all huffing and puffing and training for the heavenly Olympics.

Who are we trying to impress?

It's time to unravel the smart business suit and knit up something more homely.

The following stories tell what we did in homemade churches in New Zealand and why we did it. These stories have little or no scripture references in them as there are enough books emerging that deal with the doctrinal justification for house churches. Neither are they intended as yet another model to follow, but rather are a right-brained attempt to provoke thinking people into re-examining current teachings and traditions.

Let's stop competing in shows and instead start building relationships in make-it-up-as-you-go, homemade churches.

Homemade Church

The Vision

Psalms 127:1
*Except the Lord build the house,
they labor in vain that build it.*

Visions are not born in a vacuum, environmental factors are at work in the birthing of an idea. It was the year 1999 and YK2 rumors had reached even our ears. Things had to be pretty big to filter through our lifestyle of no television, little radio and spasmodic newspaper reading. By June 1999, the world was dividing into three categories. Those who did nothing, those who did something, and those who prepared to outlast the end of civilization. Ian and I fell into the last category. We had our hundred cans of baked beans, a sack of dried chick-peas, fresh drinking water, a camp cooker, and six dozen candles.

We also had a big red FOR SALE sign up in our

front yard. There were two reasons for the sign. New Zealand is a long and skinny land, and in many places, there are only three major arteries that circulate traffic. Our house was positioned on the middle artery, and we figured if any trouble was to arise, rioters would come down from the North, right past our house. As we had four young children, we felt vulnerable. The second reason was our kids needed more space to roam than our town yard provided.

In addition, 1999 was also a time of great unhappiness at our last church. We were looking for land and a solution to our church problem. We found the perfect property quickly. Rose Bank was a rambling old house on ten acres, thirty minutes from the city. That was the land problem solved, or so we hoped. We turned our attention to the church. We were sitting by the fire mulling over the dismal situation one evening when a radical thought dropped into Ian's head.

"We could start an outreach."

It was a new idea, but I did not skip a beat.

"Yes, and I know where," I said (thinking of my childhood home) "up Mount Tiger. The prayer group that Mum goes to have been praying for a work of God up there for fifteen years."

"Let's call your parents and see what they think," said Ian.

I glanced at the clock. "No, it's too late they will be asleep, we will have to wait until tomorrow."

The next morning Mum was sitting with Dad in bed,

Homemade Church

a cup of tea in hand, when words just popped out of her mouth, "We have been praying for a church up here for fifteen years, let's pray Now Is the Time LORD."

"Good idea," said Dad.

So together they prayed. They finished praying at 7.30am just as Ian picked up the phone and dialed.

After we all got over the wonder of the timing, Mum, and Dad, Ian, and I got down to practicalities.

The first issue was, where shall we meet?

"Perhaps someone has an unused barn we could rent," said Ian.

"That's possible," said Mum. "I'll hang a notice on the front fence and ask around."

I had great faith in Mum's ability to track down anything, especially in a farming community. If there was a suitable building within a ten-mile radius Mum would find it. She hunted wide and far but alas, found nothing.

Ian and I were also having trouble. Every month the year 2000 got closer. We needed to sell our house, but a buyer was as evasive as a barn. We stockpiled another hundred cans of food, two dozen boxes of matches and put up more FOR SALE signs.

"I think the solution to the barn problem is to build one," said Dad at last. "We have plenty of land."

"Harold do you think you would be up to it?" said Mum looking anxious. "You are not young anymore and we have only just finished building the beach house."

"I have one more building in me, and Ian can help,"

said Dad confidently.

"Where would you put it?" I asked excitedly.

"At the top of the driveway in the horse paddock," said Dad. "I'll draw up the plan this week."

Before long he was ready to build. As he removed the turf for the foundations, a great buzz of interest flew up around us. Many from The-Parent's-church wanted to help. One man even purchased secondhand windows for the new chapel.

There was so much support Ian and I felt superfluous.

"I thought we were meant to start a church but perhaps we got it wrong," said Ian. "We aren't really needed."

"Yeah, maybe we are supposed to help with the little one across the road from Rose Bank," I said.

We died on the idea of starting a church and drifted off.

The flurry of activity at Mount Tiger lasted for a few weeks and then bit by bit, everyone from The-Parents-church lost interest. Mum and Dad also lost interest. They realized the chapel was too close to their house for comfort and they were too old to host it. The bald building area greened over with grass again and Dad decided to use the second-hand windows for a glasshouse. The vision fell to the ground and lay buried for three months.

Meanwhile, our house had still not sold. As the days of waiting turned into months, Rose Bank did not seem so perfect or desirable anymore.

Homemade Church

Our house was up for sale

Wendy Hamilton

Moreover, the church across the road turned out to be a dead dinosaur. We went and had another look at Rose Bank and suddenly our whole direction changed. I rang Mum.

"We've gone off Rose Bank."

"No!" (by which she meant yes.)

"Yeah, we went and had another look at it and I don't think it is right. Besides, if it was, we would have sold by now."

"You could go back to the idea of taking some of our land," said Mum.

"We have been over this years ago. It wouldn't work sharing a driveway Mum," I said. "I know you. You are too highly strung to cope with it."

"Yes, I could," said Mum uncertainly.

"No, you couldn't," I said firmly. Suddenly I had an inspiration. "But if we took the steep land at the back, and put in a separate driveway at the other end of the property, that would work," I said thinking out loud.

"Yes, that would work," said Mum in excitement.

"And we could resurrect the idea of a Mount Tiger Chapel. If it was way over there, you won't even see it."

"That's right," said Mum, "and you two are young enough to run it. Dad and I could manage a supporting role."

Suddenly everything clicked into place. I knew the exact position for the new building. We would keep our house in town and use the shed as a chapel and a weekend cottage. When we put the idea to Dad and Ian,

Homemade Church

they were in total agreement. In August, four months before the dreaded YK2, the first bulldozer began work carving out the new driveway.

Wendy Hamilton

The Birth of the Mount Tiger Chapel

Mathew 28:19
Go ye therefore and teach all nations, baptizing them in the name of the Father, and of the Son, and of the Holy Ghost.

Thankfully YK2 was a non-event. New Year's Day 2000 was the beginning of a new century and the start of the Mount Tiger Chapel. Mount Tiger is a rural area in Northland New Zealand. The road runs along the ridge of a series of hills. On either side, there are spectacular views of dramatic forest-clad land and glimpses of the Pacific Ocean. It is very beautiful. The Chapel, however, was not beautiful and it was not anything like a normal chapel.

For a start Ian and I personally owned it. We paid for

Homemade Church

it with the money we had aside for updating our van. Ian and Dad labored throughout November and December, and by January, the shell of a building stood at the end of a long driveway. It was a little boxy structure with a gabled roof. The main room was the size of a two-car garage.

Three tiny rooms opened directly off one side, we called them bedrooms but in reality, sleeping closets was a better description. Each bedroom had a built-in bunk bed that stretched from wall to wall. It was possible to step inside the room and clean it by pivoting. The Chapel's official title was SHED FOR TRACTOR, and the two large front doors were wide enough to admit one.

On the morning of our first service, we spread an old carpet square over the concrete floor and placed thirty-two plastic chairs on top.

The walls were lined with sheetrock and the rafters showed plainly above the non-existent ceiling. There was no running water, no electricity and a bucket-in-an-outhouse type of bathroom. I

n preparation for a cup of tea at the end of the service, Mum purchased thirty-two cups, and a large container of drinking water stood next to a gas camp cooker on a short countertop.

Now in case you get the impression this is normal standards for New Zealand, let me hasten to explain it is only a little less radical than doing the same thing in North America.

Wendy Hamilton

The Chapel was not beautiful

Homemade Church

We had advertised the opening of the Chapel months prior to the event, by means of a hunk of plywood hanging from the front wire fence. In bold letters and wobbly brush strokes, Mum spelled out our vision for a community chapel. We knew every neighbor for a radius of two miles. The community was stable and many of the relationships were over thirty years old. We had gathered together many times for birthdays and New Year's celebrations at Anne and Gilbert Templeton's home. There amid the food, booze, and fireworks, Mum (who was an evangelist from the age of eleven) would corner someone and tell them they needed to get right with the Lord or they would go to hell. When the crowd got wind of it, they rolled their eyes and cracked jokes.

"Aw Anne, quit Bible bashing and leave him alone," yelled Norton.

Mum fixed him with her good eye and bawled back, "you just watch it Norton or I'll come over there and Bible bash you instead!"

They all loved Mum, they overlooked the religious quirk because they knew she loved them to bits and was such fun. When Mum walked in, the party took off. Without the booze, Mum managed to give the impression of swinging from chandeliers.

Even with such a great rapport, we did not know if any would come to the new chapel. Our neighbors were mostly farmers or small landowners, they eyed Mum's notice warily at first, worried that we might try to squeeze them for funds. But as the weeks rolled

Wendy Hamilton

by and the building arose with no hint of a collection bag rotating about the neighborhood, they relaxed somewhat. A few even expressed their admiration for our Community Spirit and thought it might be very beneficial for the Jones, or Taylors, or Blogs. In fact, they thought the whole community needed it, except themselves of course.

So, there we were, New Year's Day 2000, as prepared as possible under the circumstances.

Invitations had gone throughout the neighborhood.

Would anyone come?

A speaker was ready to give his testimony.

Would anyone come?

A large jug of water for tea was heating on the camp cooker.

Would anyone come?

Mum and I tuned our guitars (we both knew four chords.)

Would anyone come? Three minutes to eleven, A car, another car, then a couple of heads popped up at the end of the gravel driveway. They were coming! In ones, or twos, or small groups, they trickled through the gate; thirty-two unsaved neighbors and friends were coming down our long potholed driveway. We rushed out to meet them in excitement and joy, kissing some, hugging some and welcoming all.

In a little unfinished building,
On the top of a hill,
In the middle of nowhere,

Homemade Church

Run by nobodies,
Down under the bottom of the world,
A homemade church was born.

Wendy Hamilton

Sitting in Hot water

Revelation 18:4
And I heard another voice from heaven, saying, Come out of her, my people, that ye be not partakers of her sins, and ye receive not one of her plagues.

I do not like big changes. I guess I'm pretty normal in this respect. To play with the decor of a room is one thing, to sell that room and shift houses is quite another thing. There has to be a powerful reason to compel me into all that upheaval. I'd sooner stay put and potter about with wallpaper.

To move us out of the little church we had attended for nine years, it had to get horribly hot. We did not want to leave. We did not want the upheaval of change. People on the way out of a church alter their seating patterns. If they sit right up front, they are well bonded with the church. Steady progress towards the back, row by row, week by week, is a sign of progressive detachment. The

Homemade Church

next retreat once the back row is reached is Children's Church. Volunteering to help with Sunday School to escape the sermon comes just before flight.

When we first attended Last-Church, we crept in the door and slunk in the back row. We were recovering from an abusive church experience that resulted in a thriving church quickly dwindling to twenty members. We were wary and nervous about committing ourselves. The Pastor was a blind man with an outrageous sense of humor. Little by little he won our confidence and love. Each week we sat a row closer to the front. Eventually, we took regular possession of the pew behind the front seat reserved for kids. We became strongly bonded, loved the people, and were happy.

After a few years, we changed cities for ten months so Ian could go back to University. While we were away, our beloved pastor left and Golden Boy took his place. Golden Boy was the pride and joy of Last-Churches' denomination. He was handsome, smart, seminary trained and looked like a wholesome family man. He was also a bully. He emotionally abused anyone he perceived as weak. He particularly honed in on single women.

We sat in our customary seat on our homecoming Sunday. But as time went by, we started to see through Golden Boy; accordingly, we sat closer and closer to the door. Finally, it got so bad we called a special meeting to have Golden Boy removed. After much trouble, he left. The whole church heaved a sigh of relief, and we shifted forward to the second row of seats again.

For eighteen months we had no pastor and it was wonderful. There were no young Christians at Last-Church so we shared the preaching and jobs between us. Although Last-Church was small, without the wages of a Pastor the money built up and we were able to give large amounts away to Christian charities.

Eventually, the ruling powers of Last-Church felt we couldn't possibly function without a college-trained professional, so they sent us a missionary from America.

"Tom and Judy are lovely people," I said to Ian, "why do I resent them so much?"

"I feel like my parents have shifted into our home and are telling me how to brush my teeth," said Ian.

"Yes, that is exactly it," I agreed. "We never get off the milk of the word and they try to micromanage our lives."

"We are not the only ones struggling," said Ian, "have you noticed nobody sits up the front anymore?"

"That's true," I said. My mouth drooped, "they are nice people but the joy and spontaneity we had when there was no pastor, has gone." Ian nodded as I added, "I often feel trapped."

We stayed put and eventually learned to cope.

After a year, Missionary Pastor and family went back to America and Australian Pastor and family arrived. Australian Pastor started by introducing flaky ideas into Last-Church. All sorts of strife, tensions, and undercurrents arose. We sat in the back row.

Homemade Church

"How can we ride this out?" I wailed.

"We are in the inner circle and know too much," said Ian. "If we don't know what's happening, we might be able to stick it out."

We pulled off the Board and took on Children's Church. For a time, the strategy worked, Every Sunday we escaped the tedium and tension of the preaching, by teaching the kids. We had fun making popcorn, acting out Bible stories, coloring in pictures, and singing. The kids loved it and it grew. But alas, we were not allowed to enjoy our sanctuary. Assistant Pastor correctly discerned we were hiding in Children's Church and ferreted us out.

"It's not right," she said, "you are missing out on the service. I'll take over your class so you can enjoy the blessings of the pastor's teaching."

My face turned the color of old cheese and I smiled weakly as we trailed reluctantly back into the Sanctuary.

It is astonishing how the tension of one morning a week can permeate the entire week. Our sleeping took on a predictable pattern. It went like this.

Sunday night. Lots of agitated late night talking, lots of tossing and turning, little sleep.

Monday night. More agitated talking, more tossing and patchy sleep.

Tuesday night. Less talking, less tossing, better sleep.

Wednesday night, chatting, reasonably good sleep,

Thursday night, great sleep.

Wendy Hamilton

Friday night, nervous talk; anticipating the coming Sunday and patchy sleep.

Saturday night. Agitated talk, restless sleep, around the circuit we go again.

Our church attendance became erratic.

"I can't work out which is worse," I wailed to Ian, "suffering through Sunday or the where-were-you? phone call I get on Monday if we don't go? I feel trapped and oppressed."

"Yeah," agreed Ian, "I wish we could sit in the foyer. I haven't got anything out of church for years."

"Oh, don't you remember," I quoted in a sarcastic tone, "you don't go to church for what you get out of it but for what you can give to it."

"Huh, so much for that. Now they have put an end to us serving; even morning tea and cleaning is strictly controlled."

"Oh, we can still serve, the church will never say no to money," I said grinding my teeth. "They are always squeezing us for money."

The end came with the introduction of un-biblical doctrine and practices. We stood against them and won, as the new ideas were totally against the constitution of Last-Church. That evening Assistant Pastor came around to our house.

"Why don't you trust the Pastor and me," she said bursting into tears.

It was the finish. I quit church altogether and Ian took the kids to the only church in the town we hadn't

Homemade Church

tried. And somewhere, during that horrible time of upheaval, beginning with Golden Boy, we bought thirty-two plastic chairs and started Mount Tiger Chapel. Now once a month, in a little unfinished shed, on the top of a hill, we sat in plastic chairs, right in the very front row.

Wendy Hamilton

The Elephant in the Church

Jude 4:4
For there are certain men crept in unawares, who were before of old ordained to this condemnation, ungodly men, turning the grace of our God into lasciviousness, and denying the only Lord God, and our Lord Jesus Christ.

It is hard to ignore an elephant in the room, and yet, as Christians, we go to elaborate efforts to pretend that the elephant eating the alter flowers does not exist. Elephants seldom enter fully grown. They slip in, while they are still tiny. Because we are not expecting an unclean elephant, it is possible to believe the Pastor, when he says "you are wrong, there is no elephant."

It is hard to ignore the truth. Nevertheless, for the sake of peace and fear of pride, I try.

"Wendy that is not an elephant, it is a lamb," I speak

Homemade Church

the words out loud hoping to readjust my vision. After all, it must be a lamb, bought in for the nativity play. "Of course, that's it! I saw a lamb. A little pet lamb, not an elephant after all."

But the next Sunday the elephant has grown bigger than a dining table.

"Sister Joy, do you see the elephant in the room?" I ask tentatively.

"Whatever are you talking about?" Sister Joy tiptoes carefully around the elephant. "That's the donkey for the Easter play!"

"A donkey! Are you sure? It looks more like an elephant to me! Are you quite certain that's a donkey?"

She sidesteps the question. "The Pastor says it's a donkey."

"Funny looking donkey, but I guess he knows the difference between a donkey and an elephant better than me," I concede.

For a week or two, I pretend I see a donkey. But the Sunday the elephant takes the collection bag in its big trunk, it sure looks like a mamma elephant to me.

"Brother Bob, what's that elephant doing with the money bag?"

"What elephant? That's a New-Wineskin-Angel, Wendy. You need to get your eyes checked."

Eye checks involve a series of heart-searching, self-doubting, and self-condemnation as I attempt to convince myself the elephant in the room does not exist. This continues until the elephant has grown so big it is standing on my toes and crushing me into the wall. I notice people who have been coming for years have quietly slipped away. Suddenly I cannot deny the truth any longer.

"It is an elephant That is not a little lamb!"

"Sister, we don't want to hear words like that! You need to repent of your critical spirit and anti-authority, rebellious attitude! You do not see an elephant, because there is no elephant in the room!"

Our church friendships were shallow and tense as we skirted around taboo subjects for fear of gossiping. Because everybody knows, if you do see a giant elephant in the church, you ought to keep silent and only speak to God about it, especially if the elephant is in leadership.

When we left the church, we felt alone and lonely. Mount Tiger started as an outreach, but as time went on, it evolved a dual purpose. It was an outreach and a puncture repair kit. We uncovered by accident, a whole epidemic of people gored by elephants, many of whom were unshakable pillars of the church. These stable Christians of diverse denominations were actually lonely elephant watchers.

"I've attended my church for twenty-five years but I have no real friends," I heard from many.

"I struggle with the increasing worldliness in my church," said others.

"My church is more interested in following business principles than the Bible," said another. "There is no real fellowship, now you even have to pay for coffee

Homemade Church

and tea after the service."

They were bored, burdened, and oppressed by over programming. They came to Mount Tiger to give their testimony and returned the next month and the next, drawn by the fellowship and freedom. They were only hanging in at their church because they didn't know what else to do. Like us, they had tried all the churches, and knew what they were searching for was not in a standard church. These people were not weak, young, or back-sliders. They were solid Christians of twenty or more years, deacons and elders.

"This dissatisfaction with the church is much bigger than us," I said to Ian. "It is widespread."

"Yes, and not just laymen. Even some Pastors have had enough and are leaving."

"I know," I said, "Pastors are not the enemy, many of them are trying really hard. It's the system that stinks."

"Yeah," said Ian, "I'd hate to be a Pastor, people's expectations are tough on them and their families.

"We are not alone after all," I said thoughtfully.

"No, we are not alone," agreed Ian, "we are on the cutting edge of a new move of God."

Wendy Hamilton

The Ways of Animals, children, and Men

Matthew 23 8- 11

[8] But be not ye called Rabbi: for one is your Master, even Christ; and all ye are brethren. [9] And call no man your father upon the earth: for one is your Father, which is in heaven. [10] Neither be ye called masters: for one is your Master, even Christ. [11] But he that is greatest among you shall be your servant.

The dream of most New Zealand men is to own land. Generally, they start out with a quarter-acre plot and a house. If fortune smiles, they can convert a midlife crisis into a small hobby-farm, and no house. When my father turned thirty-eight, he bought forty acres.

A farm (even a toy-sized one,) needs animals. Dad

Homemade Church

chose cattle because he understood cattle. Back in his childhood when a full pail of milk weighed half his body weight and the cow stood twice his height, it had been his job to mind and care for the family house-cow. My sisters and I were nervous about the coming cattle. We imagined big bulls, but the fourteen steers who stumbled off the truck were adorable. They stared at us through their big, black, eyes and stole our hearts. We named them and got to know all their ways. There was Carrot King who loved carrots, Puzzle who always looked faintly surprised and Horns who we felt sorry for. Poopsey was a real character. He was the one who broke fences and led the rest into trouble.

We played with them and got to understand their pecking order from the top dog (or rather, Bullock) to the bottom beast and all the grades in between. We never questioned this dynamic, because intuitively, we understood natural order, as did every kid.

From popular Catherine to shunned Alisha we all knew our place, and woe betide the teacher who made Alisha class monitor instead of Catherine. We put up with it while Miss. Wilson's eye was upon us but an undercurrent of tension spread throughout the classroom, and worse than normal ugliness poured over poor Alisha at recess when the natural order reigned supreme again.

Then we broke into mini-gangs, The Populars, The Nerds, The Sporties, The Outcast's, or my group. I don't know how The Populars or The Nerds spent their forty-five minutes, but we Ordinaries had a wonderful time making huts in the school trees and acting out fairy stories and role-playing. Nobody was boss and we swapped roles amongst ourselves spontaneously; today a chief, tomorrow an Indian.

Occasionally a kid thought they were THE KING or THE PRINCESS; that King Arthur, Robin Hood or Snow White was theirs by right. When this happened, all the fluidity of the playground ground to a halt and fighting and arguing broke out. Before happy playing could resume, THE KING or PRINCESS had to be dethroned or thrown out of the game.

When I became a teenager and grew beyond Rapunzel, I attended a church run by adult 'Ordinaries.' There was no church building, no pastor, no elders, and no titles, just a little old country hall and a bunch of farmers and tradesmen.

Every Sunday our family piled into our Hillman Hunter station wagon and putted down the red gravel road to the church. On the way, we picked up Auntie Hilda. We were not related to Auntie, nobody in the district was, yet the whole community called her Auntie. Auntie was not much younger than her hundred-year-old house. It was a picturesque weatherboard cottage, set into a bush covered hillside. On spring Sundays, she clutched daffodils as she tottered down the shell path, through her cottage garden and free-range chickens. The flowers brightened the musty old hall during the church service and our homes afterward.

Homemade Church

The Service itself was kicked into gear with singing. This was accompanied by guitars and the ancient honky-tonk piano. The piano had a few keys missing and was flat in places but we did not care: Just as a wobbly rock makes an acceptable chair in a homemade game, so a flat piano and wobbly singing make acceptable worship in a homemade church.

Then Dad-the-Builder, Ray-the-Electrician or Joe-the-Road-Worker spoke. They were not eloquent men, sometimes they stumbled when they read. Nevertheless, they held our attention better than the professional preacher. For their Christianity was not theoretical. It was not learned at Seminary but through the rough and tumble of life. How to be in the world, but not of the world, was not defined by four neat points but by the day-to-day grind of refusing to conform to their drinking, swearing, blaspheming, workmates.

Old Mr. Ross, Mark, and Graham inhabited a gentler world. Their workplace was wide spaces, green fields, sunshine and hurricanes, baby lambs, and stillborn calves. When Graham spoke, it was not something rattled up that week to fill in an hour slot. It was the distilled thoughts of a month's worth of pondering as he treated his goats for foot rot and fed fish guts to his hogs.

It was a wonderful church. It was a vibrant, joyful, growing church. But alas, even when adults play, wanna-be-princesses and kings arise. Larry-the-leatherworker felt The Call and persuaded a few others to allow him to arise as The Pastor. Suddenly we had elders and deacons, church doctrine and expenses. We also had tension, fighting, and anger. All the joyful fluid sharing dried up.

Aunty Hilda's daffodils wilted.

Graham, Ray, Dad, and Dug spoke no more.

The piano clanged and the singing sobbed.

Scripture changed from a staff of comfort to a rod for beating those who resisted the new King. The homemade church tottered like a tree-hut in the wind and, eventually, collapsed. It fell on top of the ordinary folk and wounded many. The King, having lost his subjects, moved on to play with another group as an assistant King.

Many years later when we started the Mount Tiger Chapel, my father, who understood the way of animals, children, and men said, "nobody is to have a title."

So there were no official elders, no official deacons and no pastor. But we all knew right down from the eighty-year-old Cherry to four-year-old Joshua, who to go to for spiritual advice, who to go to for practical help, and who to go to for nurturing.

Occasionally a wanna-be king or princess arose, but as wanna-be kings and princesses are unwilling to function without recognition or a title, they moved away from the game peaceably and left us to continue playing spontaneously.

There is a good reason Jesus told us not to call anyone Father, Teacher, Rabbi or Master.

Homemade Church

Chapel Sunday.

Revelation 12:11
And they overcame him by the blood of the Lamb and by the word of their testimony.

The Saturday before Chapel-Sunday was a big pest and we grumbled when it rolled around. That Saturday all building projects ceased as the day was given over to a big cleanup. The whole family was enlisted to pick up bent nails, broken bricks and lumber. After the big cleanup, we transformed the building into a meeting hall. This involved, among other things, stuffing all the furniture from the main room into the three tiny bedrooms. The manhole (when we got around to building the ceiling) was big enough to stuff a warthog through.

Wendy Hamilton

We stuffed all the furniture into the bedrooms

Homemade Church

Instead, it was home to thirty-two plastic chairs. Once a month, with great huffing and puffing, we hauled them down and set them out.

In the beginning, it wasn't too bad clearing the room in readiness for the chairs. We did not stay many weekends and we did not have much furniture. But as time wore on the building projects took effect, and the ugly little building transformed into a beautiful little cottage. Bit by bit we spent more time out there and consequently our personal possessions increased. Setting up became SETTING UP, as we stuffed the bedrooms full of soft toys, crafts, a couch, a coffee table, a doll's house, a blanket box, and a hutch dresser. We used the treadle sewing machine as a podium and pushed the sofa against the back wall in an attempt to spare those bursting little bedrooms.

It was a lot of work. And every Saturday-Before, we wondered if it was worth it. We continued to wonder if it was worth it on Sunday morning, as we swept and cleaned. And we were still wondering as we busily set out teacups and cookies. We wondered right up to the moment the first car bounced down the driveway. Then we did not have time to think about anything, because we were caught up on such a carpet ride of fellowship and adventure. None of us were ever exactly sure of what would happen, and the more years we ran it, the more delightfully unpredictable it became. A whole congregation of non-Christians brings you back to basics.

Wendy Hamilton

"They don't even know Amazing Grace," said Mum after our first Chapel service.

"It was abysmal singing," I said. "They don't know any hymns or gospel songs."

"The way around it, is to start with two songs and repeat them every month and add a new one when they have got the hang of them," said Dad who had run youth groups in the past.

The idea was practical and worked well. We had another problem, however. They had no Bible knowledge at all.

"They don't even know about Jonah and the whale or David and Goliath," I said. "How are we going to teach them?"

"With Bible stories and testimonies," said Dad

So, every chapel service we had a children's story for both the kids and adults and then an ordinary Christian man gave his testimony. The services often became spontaneously interactive as we relaxed and modified. It even got quite rowdy at times. Norton and Mum were the usual culprits.

The first modification was the cup of tea after the service. Everyone enjoyed the fellowship so much they often did not go home until late. At 2 pm I frequently found myself trying to rattle up spaghetti for twenty on the little camp cooker. We decided to provide lunch. This consisted of buttered buns, a bit of baking and sausages on the barbeque. It was not gourmet, but it filled a gap and enabled fellowship to carry on through

Homemade Church

the afternoon. We never asked for food but as time wore on people started bringing yummy things and it became quite a banquet.

After lunch, our girls got their horses and gave rides to starry-eyed little girls. Our son Joe was disgusted by the lack of males his age so he prayed for boys. God answered his prayer abundantly and every month more boys turned up. There were bands of boys fishing in the creek, boys sliding down the grassy hills, boys in the bush and boys swinging off the water tower. Meanwhile, the girls continued riding up and down the driveway and the adults chattered in small informal groups. From time to time the fellowship was especially good and flowed onto dinnertime. Then we boiled the kettle again for more rounds of coffee and tea and ate the leftovers, (there were always plenty of those) before going home.

As one by one our neighbors got saved and grew spiritually, another modification was possible. We encouraged our new Christians to have a go at ministering. They started with song-leading because it was the least scary. After a few times of that, they might be ready to tell their own story of what Jesus had done for them. The Jones, Browns, and Blogs who did not come to the Chapel noticed the changes in their neighbors. Now gatherings at Gilbert and Anne's home were booze-free and baptisms happened in their hot tub.

"I'm terrified of buying a house up Mount Tiger," a local hairdresser told a friend of mine. "Everyone up there is going religious, it's like a disease. I don't want

Wendy Hamilton

to catch it."

Sometimes instead of a testimony, we acted out a Bible story. A local Emporium had scored the redundant costumes of the entire cast of the TV serial Xena Warrior Princess. For a small sum, my sister purchased a lot of Roman tunics and helmets. We borrowed them and wore them along with the traditional stripy beach towel to act out the Easter story. Because it is usually still warm in New Zealand at Easter, we did it outside and used the veranda as a stage. A small hill made a great Golgotha and the Chapel basement became the tomb. Fourteen-year-old Edward read the crucifixion account out of the Bible, while the actors interjected improvised lines where they saw fit.

The best one we ever did was a Christmas play where we used my sister's three lamas as camels. Ian as a wise man was gloriously arrayed in a gaudy crotchet blanket and looked faintly pope-like. (Something we all cheekily informed him of.) Dad had rigged up a star on the end of a fishing line so it moved along the veranda as it was reeled in. But eleven-year-old Marie stole the show as the angel that brought good news, by bouncing white-robed and tinsel crowded onto the veranda stage before cue. The "OOPS" and the look on her face bought the house down with laughter. There was nothing professional about our plays. In fact, there was nothing professional about any part of our house church, just a bunch of amateur Christians getting together to celebrate the Lord with food, fun, and fellowship.

Homemade Church

Bit by bit the building transformed

Wendy Hamilton

Saturday-Before Chapel was a big pest, and Monday-After saw building projects resume. But Chapel-Sunday was WONDERFUL.

Homemade Church

Fellowship without a Wage Packet.

Mathew 18:20
For where two or three are gathered together in my name, there I am in the midst of them.

The most difficult part of going from working for someone else to a business of your own, is the transition from a regular wage to...what? There is a wonderful security in turning up at a job and at the end of the month receiving a totally expected amount. A business, by contrast, requires faith. Money comes in erratically and unpredictably and seems precarious compared to the stability of wages.

When we did Church the normal way, we did Christian fellowship much like a wage packet. We turned up at Church every Sunday and had fellowship with the people who also attended. We did not look

Wendy Hamilton

for like-minded friends, if they went to the same church, that was who we socialized with, regardless of compatibility.

Occasionally we met someone who was a good match for us. More often, however, we hammered together mismatched friendships. They ran as well as a homemade car with a Holden body, Fiat wheels, van doors, sports car roof, hotrod muffler, and a peddle engine.

"Put aside your differences and strive for unity," preached the Pastor.

We all truly tried, but a peddle car engine is weak. At best fellowship was shallow and at worst uncomfortable. After nine years at Last-Church, only one friend remained after we left. There was not enough glue to hold us together.

Meanwhile, during the week our home-schooled kids were busy floating small businesses. Marie plunked a rickety table by the gate and sold jars of flowers to elderly ladies who passed by. As many schoolchildren passed our gate to and from school, she decided to expand her merchandise.

The rickety table was upgraded into a sturdy cart, and paper twists of popcorn overshadowed the flowers. When Marie and Hannah turned ten and eleven, I taught them to use a sewing machine and the art of assembly-line production.

Antoinette called around one morning just as the girls put the finishing touches on twenty rag dolls.

Homemade Church

The popcorn cart

Wendy Hamilton

"These are really good," said Antoinette, picking up a doll Marie had just finished. "They are good enough to sell in a real shop."

Marie and Hannah beamed.

"I don't think everything will fit on the popcorn cart," I said, eyeing the pile on the table.

"You could sell them at the Church Fair," teased my sister.

"We've quit, we are not going back."

"Really," she said, her eyebrows shooting up. "I knew you were unhappy, but I didn't think you would quit."

"We have had enough."

"Where are you going to go?"

"Nowhere," I said firmly.

"Nowhere?"

"That's right. Apart from Mount Tiger Chapel of course."

Antoinette fiddled with the doll's dress as she mulled over this startling information.

"You are right, these are good enough to go in a shop," I said changing the subject. A lightbulb lit up in my head. "We could turn my front room into a shop for a few weeks before Christmas. The house is in a good location for a shop."

"Ooh, that's a wonderful idea," said Antoinette catching the vision. "But how will you fill it? You'll need more stuff than the girls have made."

"You and I could sell stuff too," I said. "We can

Homemade Church

make country crafts, quilts, folk art, and stuff.

"Don't forget handmade soap," said Antoinette, "soap would sell well."

"Yeah, it would. Let's do it," I said.

So, for seven weeks before Christmas, I transformed the front room of our 1920s bungalow into a shop.

"Do you think anyone will come in," I asked Antoinette dubiously on our opening morning.

"Hopefully the sign will grab people's attention," said Antoinette.

I stared out the window at the large Christmas tree sandwich-board Dad had made for us and hoped she was right. As I looked, a car zoomed past, screeched to a halt and reversed to my gate. A middle-aged woman with braces on her teeth, and dressed in designer clothes, got out and clomped up the veranda and into the shop.

"I did not think a place like this existed in New Zealand," she said, her eyes going big with wonder as she stared around.

She was the first of many that dropped in. We had a wonderful seven weeks and the next year I felt God impress on me to do it again. This time I enlisted the help of my Christian neighbor, Julia.

As a money-making business, the shop was useless. But as a fly trap for fellowship, it was fantastic. We read the bible verse, where two or three are gathered there I am in the midst of them, and think, if he turns up for two or three, how much more he would turn up for two or three thousand! Wrong! We need to get down to two or three before anything really meaningful happens.

Fellowship started happening in our shop. Often it was Christian friends who popped in for a chat and a cup of tea. We were seldom busy and we had plenty of time for 'church' out the back at the kitchen table where we encouraged and prayed for one another. Then there were the Christians we had never met before. When they walked in, the Holy Spirit witnessed within each of our hearts that this was a fellow believer. Often, we stood for two hours between the rag dolls and the soap, engrossed in conversation about the Lord, before getting to the kitchen table. Sometimes they were local people, but not always. They came from all over the country and even overseas. With each encounter, there was a special God anointing, like being encased in a soap bubble with another believer. I saw how the persecuted church could operate, we did not have to look for fellowship or connections, God organized everything. Church happened spontaneously, sometimes in our shop and other times between the supermarket aisles. Once I learned to relax and ride the wind of the Holy Spirit, the fellowship was exhilarating.

Even more thrilling were the countless opportunities to share about Jesus with nonbelievers. Years earlier God had asked me to lay down my desire to see people come to Jesus. I had never heard anyone being asked to do such a thing. It flew in the face of all my thinking and church training. As part of Christianity we all need to evangelize, but here was the Lord telling me to lay

Homemade Church

it down! So, I laid it down. Saving souls became his business and I became like a little child just having fun with life, like a kid in a great big sandbox her father has made. As I stopped concerning myself with seeing people saved, odd things started happening.

"I don't know what is going on," said a woman walking in one day. Her eyes were glazed and she looked bewildered. "I was walking past and it was if my legs were taken over. I had no intention of coming in but here I am."

Another woman said, "I was driving past and I was compelled to turn the car around and come here."

Another said, "there is a large angel standing on your front veranda."

People experiencing a touch from God usually ended up sitting on the window seat. One woman was even healed of back pain while she sat.

Of course, we told them who that compelling someone was. We were allowed to do that, and some people gave their hearts to the Lord. At times I felt like a doctor with an invisible receptionist, booking appointments. Some days there would be back-to-back divine encounters, never overlapping; perfect timing. But other days if I was tired and not up to it, nothing happened.

A woman stands out in my memory. She clomped onto the veranda and slid in through the door one wet day.

"I was walking past and something drew me in," she

said.

"That often happens, Jesus sends people here," I said. "Would you like a cup of tea,"?

She nodded as she sank down on the window seat. Nobody came in as she unburdened her heavy heart to me; tears trickling down her cheeks while the rain trickled down the window pane. She desperately needed someone to listen. When she was talked out, I asked if I could pray for her. She nodded, so I prayed. When I had finished, she sat there for ten minutes, eyes tightly shut, her lips moving in a silent prayer to Jesus (maybe her first prayer.) I drew a map to Mount Tiger and suggested she come along. The next Chapel Sunday there she was.

Right from the start the Mount Tiger folk drew her into their midst and ministered to her. Some shared their testimonies, Sharon gave her a book, Bruce gave her a Bible and Andrea prayed with her, while Rebeca got her lunch. It was like watching an orchestra with an unseen conductor, now the violins, now the flutes. The final notes were played by the trumpets and big bass drums as all the men got behind her car and pushed it out of the mud. She was not a local person and we never saw her again, but I know she had a touch from Jesus.

Through a once-a-month homemade church, the shop, and ordinary day to day encounters, God faithfully provided us with fellowship. The idea that fellowship is only found by going to church is bunkum. It is as silly as saying wages are the only way of getting money. What is more, nobody becomes a billionaire on wages.

Homemade Church

The shop

Wendy Hamilton

Puffer Fish

1 Corinthians 14:34
Let your women keep silence in the churches: for it is not permitted unto them to speak.

When I was a child, my parents owned a beach house. We went there every school holiday. On wild wet days when my mother was sick of us kids fighting, she bundled us up in jackets and marched us down to the beach. We moaned and fussed at this inhumane treatment until we got in sight of the pounding waves. They were awesomely magnificent, but the greatest excitement was what they threw up. There were shells and driftwood of course, but also rope, half a fishing net, a child's plastic bucket, a dead seagull, and occasionally, a pufferfish.

Pufferfish, (for those of you who have never seen one) are the punk rockers of the fish world. Think large

Homemade Church

spikes all over a pale, yellow, fish-body. Then blow him up like a balloon in your mind and you have a pufferfish. Some bright spark in the tacky seventies had a novel idea of making them into lampshades.

When the sea of life threw Ian up onto my beach, I started to notice a similarity between men and pufferfish. Not that I am suggesting he looks like a pufferfish or should be made into a lampshade, but he did have the tendency to swell out his chest a bit when showing off before females. In those days he had a lot to learn about girls, and he resorted to ploys like stealing a pink raspberry bun from my fingers and chomping a huge bite out of it. Now I am guessing, looking back from the vantage of twenty-two years of marriage, that the intent of the bun stealing pufferfish was that I should deeply admire his quick sleight of hand and the large, manly hole left in my bun. Alas, being inexperienced in the ways of the male ego at that time of my life, I missed these subtleties and was merely annoyed.

Now that I have two sons, I have observed pufferfish tendencies start very young. It is important not to stick sharp pins in the balloon of the male ego. I have seen a few men whose womenfolk took a pin to them, and it is not good. A normal fully inflated pufferfish is amusingly attractive. But a popped puffer is sad and not even useful for a lampshade.

Naturally, a non-Christian pufferfish is more fragile than a Christian one. (After all, he doesn't have the internal security of Jesus.) With this in mind, only men

Wendy Hamilton

gave their testimonies at Mount Tiger Chapel. Once a month we had a manly man with manly muscles give his testimony in a manly voice. Men's testimonies are not better than women's testimonies. They do, however, keep the big puffer fish and all the little up-and-coming pufferfish fully inflated.

A wise woman knows that some things are more important than superficial equality.

Homemade Church

Hot Air Balloons and the Woman's Voice.

Genesis 2:18
And the Lord God said, it is not good that the man should be alone, I will make him an help meet for him.

Nearly everyone has at some stage of their life, fantasized about riding in a hot-air balloon. When our girls where little we lived in Hamilton, a city famous for hosting the Great Hot-Air Balloon Show. One week every year, hundreds of balloons took to the air, poker-dotting the sky with flamboyant colors. That was the week we stayed outside and developed a crick in our neck. One glorious afternoon, a balloon passed so low over our house we could see the man in the basket. That night we went to the source of all that sky ornamentation; a football field covered with baskets attached to elongated balloon bladders. Lying on the ground, the balloons did not look impressive. More like the dead squid heads fishermen sometimes have lying about their boats. Then the gas blasted in, and they puffed and wobbled, like air mattresses blowing up. As they rose higher and higher their individual shapes and characters became more obvious. Some were just conventional shapes but others filled out into Snoopy or Garfield.

Just as nearly everyone has fantasized about taking a balloon ride, most people fantasize about getting married at some stage of their life. Marriage and a hot-air balloon ride have a lot in common. Men are the balloon, but without a good woman in the basket blasting the warm air of trust and confidence in them, most men lie on the ground like a dead squid.

I've heard that mother alligators incubate their eggs by piling rotting vegetation over them. They can tell (I guess they have women's intuition too) how many leaves to heap on or remove to keep the temperature just right for healthy growth. So too, a good wife intuitively knows how to heap on or withhold praise, so that her balloon soars into the sky. Not enough results in no lift-off. But praise, without truthful checks, could cause him to combust. Like a balloon, a good marriage can carry heavy loads high over mountains.

My Grandmother used to say "man is the head and woman is the neck that turns the head."

Homemade Church

We laughed at this, but she was right.

Grandma and Grandad were Redding Brethren; a particularly legalistic type of church denomination. Every week all the ladies trotted off to church with their heads submissively covered and sat silently through the service. Demure they might have been, but cowed under and voiceless they were not. I never met a Brethren woman who did not ooze confidence and strength.

As Grandma said "The men would announce a subject for next week's discussion. During the week their wives gave them their advice."

This is not to imply that the men were squids on the ground without opinions. Rather that they talked things over and gained confidence from their womenfolk. Of course, by the time they got to the meeting they probably thought all ideas were entirely their own. Every woman has had the experience of blowing a hot idea into her balloon, only to receive a cold blast back. Two days later, however, suddenly he has a brilliant idea that looks suspiciously familiar.

This happened to me only the other week, but I won't divulge the details, as my own hot-air balloon will be reading this and I do not want to weaken my position. A woman's strength is letting him believe he thought it up all by himself. It is not that hot air balloons are jealous of ideas. It is the natural result of thinking like a slow-cooker. A woman's intuition works like a microwave. Her cup of water has boiled while he is still warming up his ceramic bowl. Two days later ting, a GREAT IDEA

Wendy Hamilton

has been born, ready for next week's meeting.

An hour was all the time the hot air balloons at Mount Tiger Chapel had pre-eminence. Afterward, over lunch and during the afternoon, the men spoke their ten-thousand-words each, while we women effortlessly outstripped them with our twenty-five-thousand. Considering our verbal advantage, an hour's handicap is light, and a small price to pay for a glorious balloon ride.

Homemade Church

Passing on the Baton.

1 Corinthians 11:1
Be ye followers of me, even as I also am of Christ.

My father taught me to read. Once a week he brought home, a new reader and I bounced up and down with excitement as we labored through Janet and John. My father was not a particularly fluent reader, he would stumble a bit himself, but I only worked that out when I reached the ancient age of eight. Mum was the better one at reading Cinderella aloud. It was Mum who taped words about the house. Each sign proclaimed boldly in crayon, chair, table, door, etc, and dangled off the appropriate chair, table, or door. I dare say I had plenty of reading lessons at school but I don't remember one.

I had plenty of lessons in sports during the many

Wendy Hamilton

years I plodded through school. Soccer, rugby, and (my all-time hatred) netball. Every week we huffed and puffed up and down the field or court in our pumpkin-shaped romper pants. It was horrible, and I developed a strategy of rushing around as far away from the ball as possible. A few times my cunning failed and I actually had to (horror of horrors) touch the dreaded round thing. Then the whistle shrilled and the umpire yelled "penalty." Once again, I had transgressed some vital law that, despite years of instruction, I failed to grasp.

Both my sisters showed the same ineptitude. I found out much later all my cousins and aunties and uncles on Dad's side of the family shared the problem of tennis rackets with invisible, ball-shaped holes. Auntie Rosemary confided in me how embarrassing she found her husband when her side of the family got together. Cousins Lynette and Joe quietly slunk away when the softball bat and bases came out. Not so their father. He was out there swinging wildly, while his wife wilted with shame. Uncle Ernie did not care. He was a strong extrovert and any center stage was just fine with him. He was a great storyteller and at our family reunions, he had us crying with laughter as he recounted stories. Wild, true stories, like the time he scavenged a rotary hoe from the dump and carried it home on the back of his motorbike. Our ancestors were ingenious at scavenging and recycling.

"No better place for a picnic than the dump," was a sacred family saying handed down through the

Homemade Church

generations.

"Half a trailer-load to the dump and a full load home," was another.

To us, the dump was a place of provision and inspiration. Furniture, tools, and material for building projects often came home from the dump. My father's generation all built beach cottages out of demolition stuff. My sisters, cousins and I never once had a lesson on building or recycling, but most of us build beach houses or mountain cabins out of demolition materials, unconsciously carrying the baton into marriage and the next generation.

My family has an even deeper heritage. We come from a long line of men and women of faith. For at least six generations (who knows how many more), they loved and served the Lord. Even in the desperate days when Robert and Andrina, fresh from the Shetland Isles, labored to hack out a precarious existence in the most hostile part of New Zealand, not an ax was laid to a tree on the Sabbath.

In keeping with traditions, our family was in church every Sunday. My sister Rubella had the distinction of being the youngest baby to ever lie in the crib of the Baptist nursery, while Antoinette and I toddled off to Sunday School. I don't remember one Sunday-School lesson. But I do remember the birthday ritual of standing in front of the class and reaching deep into a mysterious brown paper bag. I pulled out an eraser with the words, "For God so loved the world etc," printed on it. I credit the birthday eraser for the effortless ease I can recall John 3:16. I also remember with effortless ease, the dullness of the sermons and the long vinyl padded pews that got harder and pricklier as the morning's edification dragged on. I remember too, the rows of long lights, dangling like strung-out wind chimes and the millions of dots on the tiled ceiling that I counted to while away the time. I do not, however, remember one thing the Pastor said all those suffering Sundays.

When I became a young adult, I continued the family heritage and attended church. Of the many sermons I heard, all that remains is a one-liner from a blind Pastor. "The Lord will say well done good and faithful servant, not, good and successful servant."

Hundreds of hours compressed down to one meaningful sentence.

Like most Christian families, Mum and Dad spasmodically felt convicted over our dwindling family devotions. Once again, they tried. Once again, Dad read a passage of scripture and gave a short teaching; spiritual food to digest along with our physical food. It gave us indigestion and was a torturous end to the meal. Fortunately, it always collapsed after a few weeks and lay dormant until the next attack of parental guilt. I do not remember one point from those family devotions.

But I vividly remember the spec house. The Spec House was a house Dad contracted to build for a certain price. He won the job easily as his quote was by far the lowest. After he accepted the job, he realized he

Homemade Church

was mistaken in his calculations. In the days of writing out accounts in specially designed books, Dad added up four pages of figures, forgetting the fifth page that remained behind the fourth. He went ahead and built that house, knowing full well he was building it for less than cost because he said, "the bible says a godly man will keep his word even when it hurts him." I was six-years-old and I never forgot the lesson. I do not remember anything my father said at family devotions, but I remember everything he modeled.

Why do we persist in believing that formal teaching is the primary way to pass on the baton of faith and underestimate the power of modeling?

Wendy Hamilton

The Old Hag or the Young Lady?

Acts 17:11
These were more noble than those in Thessalonica, in that they received the word with all readiness of mind, and searched the scriptures daily, whether those things were so.

I guess most of us have seen those clever pictures at some time. The ones where depending on how you focus, you see either the old hag or the beautiful young lady. While you remain focused on the hag's face, it is impossible to see the young lady. So, it was with the church. As long as we remained in the established system, we failed to see how church could be different.

When I finally quit, I started a church fast. Food fasting is almost a lost discipline in the western church, but something that should be done regularly. Fasting is not fun. It is boring at best and miserable at worst, but

Homemade Church

oh so beneficial for the body and spirit. At the beginning of a fast, you can expect stomach cramps. Then your tongue gets white and furry and you don't smell too good as the body rushes to get rid of all the poisons it's been longing to clean out. As your stomach shrinks, the hunger cramps pass off, and you feel a lot better. Finally, your head clears and your thinking and sense of smell becomes sharper. During the fast, you may feel weakened, but the end result is stronger mental, spiritual and physical health.

Fasting church after a lifetime of imbibing is miserable. The stomach cramps of my church fast kicked in on Sunday mornings. Every Sunday, Ian took the kids off to church while I stayed at home, grappling with guilt for not going too. After a few Sundays the detoxing started.

I had accumulated a lot of poisonous beliefs and crippling religious bondages over the years. It was time to reevaluate. Christian clichés and dogmatic statements were the first up for inspection. Painstakingly all doctrine and a whole belief system had to be picked apart, reassessed, kept or discarded. This process was the dark night of the soul. Satan's accusations accompanied every question.

"You're a misfit," he whispered, "anti-authority. A little piece of coal outside the fire grows cold." And the most terrible of all, "How dare you question the validity of any prophesy or gift of the Spirit operating in the church, you Holy Spirit blasphemer!"

Wendy Hamilton

He was there in my head, wrestling with me at every turn. He came at night just before deep sleep and taunted me.

"You've lost your salvation," he sneered.

"If you confess with your mouth Jesus is Lord and believe in your heart God raised Him from the dead you will be saved," I countered, clinging to the scripture with my fingernails.

I gave my life to Jesus at age four and never doubted Jesus's love or forgiveness until one horrible night when I succumbed to the lie. It was the lowest pit. No forgiveness and a lost eternity yawned at me. Full-blown terror dropped over me in hopelessness like I had never before experienced.

"I may have lost my salvation but I will endeavor to get as many people to heaven as possible, even if I am lost," I vowed through gritted teeth.

That was the point Satan left me alone, and little by little I climbed out of the pit.

During that time, the Lord sent friends several times a week to encourage me. My head started clearing, and though I felt weak, my whole belief system had experienced a cleansing purge. My focus shifted. The hag blurred and glimpses of the beautiful young lady peeped through.

Meanwhile, Ian continued trailing miserably off to church every Sunday for the sake of the children. Eventually, I challenged him.

"Why are you going to a church?" I asked.

Homemade Church

Lazy weekends between Chapel weekends

Wendy Hamilton

"You get nothing out of it, can give nothing to it, and our children hate it? You are modeling dead traditions, not vibrant Christianity.

His head cleared too. "We will leave the church for a year as a trial run. If any of us go backward spiritually, we will return," he promised.

Suddenly church became an adventure. At that time, there were other small groups popping up. We were not the only ones dissatisfied with the institutional church. The first Sunday of the month was still Mount Tiger Chapel. Second Sunday became Hukerenui Chapel, third Sunday Dargaville, fourth, and the occasional fifth Sunday became time to catch up with other friends and small groups.

Instead of complaining about going to church like they used to, our kids complained if we decided to stay home occasionally.

It took a full year of adventure and fruitfulness like we had never experienced before we saw the viable, vibrant alternative to the institutional church. But finally, our focus shifted and we could clearly see the beautiful young woman.

Homemade Church

Horses and Water Bugs

Deuteronomy 11:19
And ye shall teach them (scriptures) to your children, speaking of them when thou sitteth in thine house, and when thou walkest by the way, when thou liest down, and when thou riseth up. And thou shalt write them upon the door of thine house and upon thy gates.

God has given us a written and visual manual to instruct us about Himself and ourselves. All Christians are (or should be) familiar with the Bible but few take notice of the instructions found in creation. Maybe it is because, in order to read the visual-manual, you have to slow down to see its lessons. You can't buy a big concordance and look up all the lessons a herd of horses can teach us about ourselves and our Creator. You actually have to spend time watching them, thinking

Wendy Hamilton

about them, meditating and pondering on the intricate way in which they relate to one another, and have the Holy Spirit illuminate your understanding. I learned how to relate to my Mother-in-law by watching my favorite mare.

Whenever a group of people new to house-churches come together, the first question is "What do we do with the children?"

I think the best answer to this question (as the Bible has only a little to say about it), is to look closely at the animal kingdom. While we are not animals, our higher powers of reasoning and ability to choose, makes us dumber than the animals sometimes. I dare say The Lord has put an exception to the rule somewhere, but generally, all immature animals are with their mothers right in the middle of the herd. Sheep do not have nurseries, cows do not have cud-chewing classes, pigs do not have youth groups, and a pack of wolves moves as one, not in age-segregated mini-groups.

I read of a herd of elephants who suffered the plight of losing all the big old bull elephants. This left an unsupervised teenage youth group. These huge hoodlums got out of control and were terrorizing all the villagers, wrecking houses and tearing up gardens. The people fixed it by importing big bull elephants into the area. These respect-commanding males traveled in crates bearing notices, "I'm off to Africa to kick butt." And kick butts they did. Problem solved.

At Mount Tiger, we talked about the idea of a separate

Homemade Church

program for the children, but unanimously we decided to keep the kids among us. It is so much easier to kick butt if the butt is sitting right next to you, rather than in the other room. Besides, how can we pass onto a boy that Christianity is a manly thing, unless that boy sees Dad sitting there highly interested and participating?

The New Zealand Department of Conservation has water health charts which they give out for free. Sometimes, the kids and I got one and tramped down to the creek at the bottom of the hill to see how many of the water bugs we could find. Lots of very tough, pollution hardy bugs, but an absence of fragile ones means the water is in bad shape. But if all the water bugs are there, even the fragile ones, the water is very healthy.

You can check the spiritual condition of a church the same way. Men and teenagers are the fragile church bugs, the first to go. Old ladies, on the other hand, are the really tough bugs. They will survive where nothing else will and are usually carried out in their coffins. Women and children are the in-between church bugs. Kids, however, are falsely represented in this group. They are only there because parental pressure has prevailed. Left to their own inclinations, kids outstrip men and teenagers as fragile bugs. Wise is the church that takes notice of these most delicate critters.

Kids are boredom barometers. They see it like it is and say it like it is. Adults tell social lies. "What a wonderful meaningful message," they say even if it was not. Kid's, however, state baldly, "That man was boring. I thought he would never shut up, my legs went to sleep, I'm hungry." If kids shuffle and make frequent trips to the bathroom, you can guarantee the adults are equally bored. If it were possible to unzip all the adult heads like pencil cases and examine their thoughts like colored marker pens, something like this is going on.

"I wish that guy would shut up."

"What! Only five minutes since I last looked at the clock."

"Oh no, I thought that was his last point, he's got another ten pages to go!"

"I must be so much more sinful and less spiritual than everyone else to have these awful thoughts."

Kids need to be in the midst of us to save us from spiritualizing boredom. If it is too long and boring for the kids, it's too long and boring for the adults. An exposition exploration of Leviticus will bring an explosion of undercover whispering, scuffling and flicking paper pellets from the boredom barometers. But watch those same barometers sit still and listen to testimonies coming from the significant adults in their lives. Just like horses, sheep, and other animals, kids need adults and adults need kids. We need to stick together and move like a healthy herd for maximum spiritual health.

Homemade Church

Sand Flies.

Ephesians 6:13
For we wrestle not against flesh and blood, but against principalities, and against powers, and against the rulers of the darkness of this world, against spiritual wickedness in high places. Wherefore take unto you the whole armor of God, that ye may be able to withstand in the evil day, and having done all, to stand.

No New Zealander remembers when they first saw the sea. Going to the beach is a New Zealand way of life. We picnic on the beach, holiday on the beach and marry on the beach. I did not understand how much of my life was orientated around the sea until we moved to Colorado. I found myself constantly scanning the horizon for water. On car trips, undulating prairie land with sparse trees made me think of sand dunes with the expectation of sea just over the next hill. I've always had a good sense of direction, but in America, it went

Wendy Hamilton

haywire; in Connecticut, it was back to front and in Colorado, nonexistent. I now realize, I unconsciously orientate myself by the sea. There are few places in New Zealand where you don't glimpse the sea spasmodically.

When I was nine, my parents bought a hump and hollow beach section. And while Dad shifted the hump into the hollow one shovel full at a time, we kids played on the beach. Ruakaka is a lovely long sweeping beach with beautiful white sand and breakers. It is a popular place; kids love the little breakers, surfies love the big ones, and adults love lazing on the beach.

Off this restless surging coast is an estuary. The estuary is lovely in a different way. It has no waves to jump over or ride on, but it is quiet enough to boat and swim in. When the tide is out, you have to cross a distance of flat sand before you get to the water. The sand appeared empty as Antoinette, Rubella and I walked over it. Then from apparently nowhere, great clouds of little tiny sand flies leaped out around us, vying for the banquet of our legs.

"Oh, these are horrible," we yelled, slapping our legs and skipping about trying to avoid them, but alas, it was impossible. They were an inevitable part of the beach. Coming back after the swim was always worse, as the saltwater on our legs heightened their itchy sting. They weren't dangerous or even that bad; they were just unpleasantly irritating. We came to ignore them and view them as simply before and after irritations, worthwhile putting up with for the wonderful refreshing

Homemade Church

swim.

Every house church we started (there have been four so far) has had its accompaniment of irritating sand flies. We have come to expect them and even rejoice in them. Just as the literal leaping pests were the sign that the refreshing water was near, the sudden poof of figurative pests, is a sign something is upsetting the devil's domain. So far these sand flies have generally materialized in three forms; health hassles, night nuisances, and day troubles.

Health hassles tend to be energy drains, headaches, and minor health problems. Night nuisances include nightmares, harassed sleep, irrational fears, and even the occasional demonic visitations. Day troubles usually take the form of nasty rumors and false accusations, often from churches and sometimes from family members. We have found the best way to deal with health hassles and night nuisances is to pray the blood of Jesus over ourselves, especially at night, and to use the name of Jesus. The day troubles are most effectively coped with by developing a thicker skin and keeping a sense of humor. (Some accusations will be quite ludicrous.) Just ignore them all and push on, and, like the literal sand flies, once you're out there swimming in the cool refreshing water they will drop off.

Wendy Hamilton

The Building Project.

Isaiah 54:2
Enlarge the place of thy tent, and let them stretch forth the curtains of thine habitations: spare not, lengthen thy cords, and strengthen thy stakes.

I had no intention when I got up that morning of buying a building. In fact, buying a building was the last thing on my mind when the phone rang.

"Hi Wend," said my sister's voice, "I've seen a little building for sale. It's the ex-club rooms of the croquet club. It's a building for relocating, going cheap at fourteen-thousand dollars because it's not a proper house. I think it might do as a temporary house while Chris builds our dream one in the paddock next to you. Do you want to come with me and have a look?"

Did I want to? I love buildings and love going out

Homemade Church

with Antoinette, of course, I wanted to. The gravel under the car tires crunched as we drew up in front of the little 1950s building. My eye took it in, in a single sweep. A simple gable roof ran the entire length of the building. It's V-shaped apex graced the narrow side-elevations. The pink front boasted two small multi-paned windows and two doors. That was all. It looked cute in a tired unassuming way.

We entered through the end door into a small unlined room and passed into the main room. A basic bench seat ran around three sides. A small kitchen with a push-up serving hatch opened off the fourth wall. What caught my eye was the expanse of windows stretching along the back and sidewall.

At that moment, it was as if the Lord's presence descended into the room. I did not see the crowd of tired old houses through the grimy windows. Instead, I saw the Mount Tiger hills.

I saw Lucy in the Kitchen handing coffee through the hatch. I saw the bench seats loaded with kids. I saw the room full of plastic chairs and a treadle sewing machine podium. I heard imaginary guitars and happy singing, a manly man with manly muscles telling how Jesus loved him, and Mum, and Norton yelling cheek at each other. The narrow wooden front door I instantly exchanged for wide multi-paned French doors opening out onto a generous deck which overflowed with phantom people, and imaginary food, a BBQ tucked in the end corner. I knew we had been getting more and more squashed in our cottage-chapel but I had not thought of another building until that moment.

"You've got first dibs on it, Sis, because you found it, but if you don't want it, I think Ian and I should buy it. It would make a great Mount Tiger Chapel No 2." I said.

"Ooo, you're right," said Antoinette. "You are welcome to it because it is no good for us. I want something more like a house."

I made a hasty phone call to Ian.

"How much money can we rake up, Darls?" I asked.

"What do you want now?" he sighed, "another chair or clock?"

"No, not this time. I want a building."

"A building? What do we want a building for?" The newness of the idea turned his voice grumpy.

"Another chapel."

He was not convinced. He thought it was a dumb idea. He thought we should just leave it. It was another one of my hair-brained ideas.

"What do you mean you think God is in this?" he demanded.

He could not be bothered looking…

It was just a sidetrack…

Yesterday we hadn't even thought of another building…

It was foolishly impulsive...

"Oh, well, alright," he relented. "But only for a few minutes after work."

Homemade Church

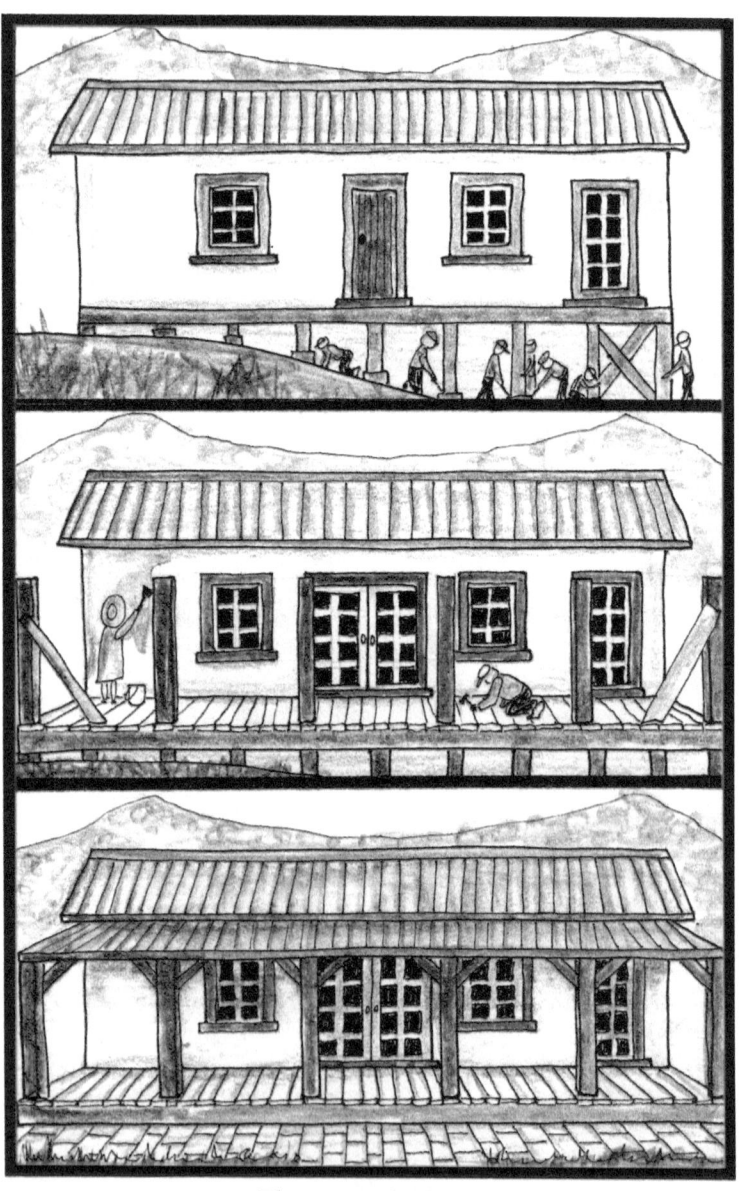

The second Chapel

Wendy Hamilton

"Oh, thank you, thank you," I gushed.
"You realize I'm only doing this to keep you happy."
"Yes," I said.
"It's a waste of time, you know?"
"Uh-huh."
He came. He looked. And he also saw the Mount Tiger Hills out the windows, Lucy in the kitchen, and felt God's presence hovering over that 1950s unassuming little building. That night he sat in the middle of the living room floor with all our bank books, check accounts and bills spread around as his fingers busily tapped at a calculator.

Back in the early days of our marriage, we handed over the expected 10% of his wage (plus offerings) to the church. But over time as the gap between our values and the churches values widened, our giving patterns changed. Each year we took on more World Vision Children and deducted the cost from the tithes the church expected to spend on new padded seats. We gave the car-park-money to Habitat for Humanity and the prayer-tower money we spent on bibles for Russia. Over the years our giving to the church dwindled, but even so, when we finally left and stopped giving to the church altogether, the extra money mounted up quite quickly. We kept a special checkbook and gave as the Lord led. It was very exciting giving all of it exactly in line with our hearts. But I digress.

At the end of all the raking and scratching and squeezing the tithe, personal savings and the New Van

Homemade Church

account (it had built up again after the first Chapel raid,) he came up with eleven-thousand-dollars; a four-thousand-dollar God Gap, as we figured we needed a thousand for permits and legal fees. We decided to offer nine thousand to allow room for bargaining. I was embarrassed to even ring with the offer. Would the Office Lady laugh at me? From fourteen thousand down to nine or ten thousand on a building that would have cost forty-five-thousand if it had been a little more like a house, was downright cheeky. It would have to be a miracle.

The miracle happened. And we did not even need to use the thousand dollar bargaining slush fund. That could go towards the new veranda. Three months and a lot of paperwork later, Mount Tiger Chapel, No 2 inched down our driveway. It was five am when the bright headlights of the huge hydraulic truck with its accompanying tractors and pilot vehicle pierced the thick blackness.

We sat up on Chapel No 1's veranda and watched everything. We particularly admired the iron nerve of the tractor driver as he pulled and slewed the huge trailer and its burden into position. He was operating confidently right on the edge of a gut-wrenchingly steep hill as if it wasn't there. Just before dawn No 2 was finally in position. As the sun rose and the light strengthened, a change came over Mr. Iron Nerves, and he paled as he saw for the first time the exact terrain he had so confidently swung around on.

Wendy Hamilton

"Cor, I'm glad I didn't know that was down there," he admitted. "I'm glad I'm finished and it's in place."

Now came the tricky process of getting the building off the trailer and onto its new foundation. We watched it all. At the morning tea break, Mum and Dad joined us. At lunchtime, Norton, Lucy, Rose, and Cherry came, Lucy, bearing goodies as she had rightly assessed I would be too excited to think of anything as mundane as lunch. We sat there and celebrated while I waxed eloquent about how cute it would look once it was lowered down onto its foundations. In my mind's eye, I saw it sitting low, tucked under the trees. The first indication a shock was on the way, was when they sent one of the guys into town for longer piles.

"Why would they want longer ones?" I said gnawing my nails. "The ones they already have look excessively long."

By afternoon tea break I saw why they wanted them and was horrified. My low-lying cute little building tucked under the trees was towering up at one end on long stilts, leaving plenty of headroom for the men underneath to walk about comfortably.

"Oh dear, I had no idea the ground sloped that much. How on earth can I make that ugly thing attractive?" I said. "It looks like a hut in Bangladesh built on stilts over a river!" I sent a quick prayer heavenward.

"Please help Lord."

A comforting thought came to me; every time something like this has happened in the past, it has

Homemade Church

worked out better in the long run. "I trust you, Lord," I whispered, "even though I don't know how you can possibly fix this one."

The men finished and left. Next week Dad and Ian started to build the new veranda (the van account had built up enough for another raid, sigh,) while I painted the inside.

We stripped the old linoleum off the floor, repaired a rotten spot, sanded it and oiled it. Then wonder of wonders, Antoinette and Chris flattened their paddock for their new house and needed somewhere to dump the excess soil.

"Bring it on over!" I said joyously.

When the bulldozer was finished, the basin of land between Chapel no 2 and the driveway had turned into a lovely flat lawn. Finally, my vision was realized.

On opening day, a long, low building sat tucked under spreading trees. Inside, the stretch of windows (just as I once visualized) faced the Mount Tiger hills. Forty-five plastic chairs were set out, the guitars were tuned and ready.

The treadle sewing machine podium was in place and a yellow ribbon stretched across multi-paned French doors. Beside the ribbon, scissors in hand, stood Cherry. The whole congregation (assembled on the veranda) listened as Walter made a speech.

"My wife brings home many things when she goes out shopping," he said, "but never once has she bought home a building!"

Wendy Hamilton

Take Off

Acts 5:42
*And daily and in the Temple, and in every house,
they ceased not to teach and preach Jesus Christ.*

I love plane rides. But the best part for me is Take Off. I buckle the seat belt excitedly anticipating the ride. The plane moves slowly, trundling out to the runway. It halts, turns, positions itself, the engines rev and whine, the plane shudders, and then it happens. She starts moving. Slowly at first, but quicker, quicker, faster, faster, more roar and shudder until I feel pushed hard back into my seat. Then the moment I've been waiting for, that slight, almost imperceptible lift as the nose tilts up. Irrationally I expect to hear a tow bar scrape on the tarmac, but no, the shuddering smooths out and we are up and looking down at Monopoly houses from tilting

Homemade Church

seats before straightening and gliding on.

Planting a house church is similar to a plane ride, and for Ian and me getting it in the air is the best part. We buckle our seat belts in nervous anticipation as we meet with one or two like-minded souls. Mount Tiger was unusual in so many coming the first morning. Looking back, I'm sure it was Gods special encouragement to boost our confidence. The next month far less came and it continued to dwindle until we got down to the worst morning of all; Ian and I, our four kids, Mum, Dad, and the speaker. We were in low spirits and Mum was embarrassed (having been the one to invite the speaker.) Nevertheless, we determined right from the start we would not worry about numbers and if it wound up just us praising The Lord, we would be faithful.

Still, it was a little difficult when the test came. But halfway through, a small miracle happened. Crystal, an unsaved neighbor, and her little girl walked in for the first time. That morning our plane trundled to the end of the runway, turned slowly and positioned itself; then it stopped. We did not know at the time, but Crystal and Peony were the revving of the plane's engine and the release of the brakes. From that morning onwards, slowly at first, but quicker, quicker, faster, faster, more and more, they came, and after about ten months, almost imperceptibly the planed lifted, smoothed out and glided on.

Just as you must have a plane if you want to fly, you need two like-minded families for a house-church, one to host and one to back up and encourage. What our family loves to do is to find others who want to have a go at a home-church but lack confidence. We run alongside like trainer wheels on the side of a kid's bike until the house-church lifts off. This can take anything from ten to twenty-one months. Then we wave goodbye, keep in touch from time to time, but move on to help launch the next church. That is our family's role and is one of the reasons we only host a house-church once a month. It gives us three Sundays a month to help launch more house-churches and gives us wider fellowship as we move around.

Other people, however, may prefer to be the pilot of a single 'plane.' They host the same church every week at their house. Both models work, it just depends on which model God has called you too.

Although many house-churches fly, some do not. Sometimes the plane merely trundles along the runway; the passengers enjoy restful scenes from the window, then it returns to the terminal. Everyone gets out refreshed and goes back to normal church life. There's nothing wrong with that either.

Whether you prefer a little trundle, lift-offs, or established trips, the ride is refreshing and worthwhile.

Homemade Church

Chrystal

Romans 12:2
And be ye not conformed to this world: but be ye transformed by the renewing of your mind, that ye may prove what is the good, and acceptable, and perfect, will of God.

The week before she and her three-year-old daughter walked into Mount Tiger Chapel, Chrystal had been to the local Tibetan Monks, and it showed.

"If anyone is bothering you, just surround them in pink," she solemnly told me. "It agitates them, and calms you."

I stared at her, nonplused by her statement. I had met Chrystal a year before when she drove unexpectedly down the driveway. The unfamiliar car crunched to a halt and the window slid down. A woman with long blond hair popped her head out.

"Do you do christenings?" she asked.

"No, but we can pray a prayer of dedication," I said.
"Oh."

She drove away and that was the last I saw of her, until now

"Pink, hmm, really?" I murmured. The Tibetan Monk logic confused me. How on earth did you surround an aggressive person in pink? I shot up a quick arrow-prayer. "Lord, how can I witness to this woman when we can't even have a normal conversation?"

"Don't worry about it," was impressed on my heart, "I can bypass all that and let her know you have something she needs."

I smiled and relaxed, "Would you like another cup of tea?" I asked taking her empty cup.

To my surprise, Chrystal and Peony kept coming. Every chapel service they were there, and we grew to love them dearly. Peony was a pretty, serious-eyed, little girl and Chrystal, a youthful-looking forty-year-old, who was smart and uncannily perceptive (when the Tibetan Monk side wasn't speaking.) She was also a dedicated mother and delighted when baby number two arrived, a beautiful healthy boy called Lewis. During labor, she experienced the power of prayer first hand and somewhere around that time she gave her heart to the Lord. As she grew spiritually, memories of her late mother seated at the piano singing hymns surfaced, along with her mother's old Bible. Because the King James translation is difficult to read, we bought her a simpler version. As she began to read the Bible, pray,

Homemade Church

and do what it said, Chrystal's thinking straightened up, and the 'pink' conversations disappeared.

This little family became the darlings of Mount Tiger Chapel, and we gathered around them as Nana Elaine, Poppa Noel, Aunty Wendy, Uncle Ian, Aunty Lucy, and Uncle Norton, etc. When it seemed that her partner had given his life to the Lord, our joy overflowed. They dedicated their children to the Lord and got married a few weeks later at Mount Tiger Chapel.

Ian and I were initially dubious about running a wedding. We were not professionals and had never done anything like that before. Moreover, although the building had advanced to look like a cute little cottage and now sported wraparound verandas, it still did not have a proper bathroom and still was small. The wedding numbers, originally predicted at twenty, swelled to eighty.

"You can use our field for parking and the barn for the reception," offered Antoinette graciously.

"That would help, but this makes me think of those seventies gags of how many bodies can you stuff in a mini?" I said nibbling my fingernails.

"It will be fine," said Chrystal confidently, "most of the guests will be too intimidated to come inside. They will probably stay on the veranda."

Perceptive as usual, Chrystal was spot on. There were plenty of vacant plastic seats inside, while the guests crammed onto the verandas and watched the ceremony through the French doors or big glass windows. Like the local hairdresser, they viewed religion as a deadly disease and were appalled Chrystal and Dalton had caught it. A Pastor friend of ours performed the ceremony, and Ian wielded a video camera about the half-empty room. Afterward, Chrystal (looking beautiful in a cream silk suit and pretty blond ringlets) leaned on Dalton's arm as they walked from the Chapel down a flower-lined path. At the end of the path was a guard of honor; two long lines of blokes and girls in leather jackets. They sat astride Harley Davidson bikes and escorted Dalton and Chrystal a hundred yards up the Chapel driveway, a hundred yards along the road, past the grassy square of slumbering car bodies, and fifty yards down Antoinette and Chris's driveway to the barn.

Inside the barn were trestle tables; maroon sheets and sprays of flowers had transformed them into a long bridal table and several buffet tables.

On them was a delightful array of savory and sweet pastries, cheesecakes, chocolate mud cakes, and a pineapple studded ham. In addition, there were deviled eggs, asparagus rolls and millions of sandwiches that Noreen and I feverishly made earlier that morning. Guests sat on sweet-smelling hay bales and ate from plates on their laps.

While we ate and socialized, Mum breathed religion germs over some of the guests, and I discovered to my delight, that the girl with luminous orange hair (she had had one of those unexpected experiences with hair dye you least want before a wedding) was a friend from my

Homemade Church

distant past.

"Would you like a drink of sparkling grape juice, Roxy?" I asked her as we reminisced over old times.

She looked at me anxiously. The lack of booze made the religion germs seem more deadly. Someone banged a glass. Ting, ting, ting, and Dalton stood up to speak. After the normal compliments to the Bride and Bridesmaids, he said,

"You are all welcome to come back to Chrystal and my house for drinks afterward."

Roxy smiled and breathed a sigh of relief.

It was a happy day. Unfortunately, not every love story has a happy ending. For a time, they got along. Alas one year and an almost fatal bike accident later, Dalton turned away from the Lord and walked away from his family.

We cried with Chrystal, prayed with Chrystal and continued to surround them with love, move furniture and fix the roof.

Dalton may have shifted out but Chrystal knows she will never be alone because she has Jesus. Although her path is still difficult, we have watched Chrystal emerge as a strong woman who walks close to God and has an obedient "yes Lord" written over her heart.

The Tibetan Monk logic has gone and is being replaced day by day with a growing Proverbs 31 wise woman, who surrounds herself and others in prayer, not pink.

Wendy Hamilton

Crystal and Dalton

Homemade Church

Changing Fashions.

Romans 12:1
Therefore, I urge you, brothers and sisters, in view of God's mercy, to offer your bodies as a living sacrifice, holy and pleasing to God, this is your true and proper worship.

Looking through family photo albums can be a painful process. The fashions that were so cool at the time look ridiculous. I cannot believe we wore glasses that big. What suspension of taste compelled us to don orange dresses and platform shoes?

A childhood photo stands out in my memory; black and white Antoinette, Rubella, and I, our mouths squashed into stiff smiles under boyish hairdos. In the photograph, we are wearing skirts with wide elastic waists. For some unfathomable reason, these are hoisted into the chest region, making us appear mostly legs,

Wendy Hamilton

but in a Daddy-Long-legs way, not a Barbie way. The fact we are clean and carrying little handbags, suggests Mum took the photo before we went to church.

Like clothes, churches, and words also pass through fashions. In the days of my childhood church was an hour-long. Singing was interspersed between the preaching. The hymn numbers were displayed ahead of time on a wooden board with slots to hold changeable numbers. The preacher spoke in a singsong, lulling rhythm. Back then the word 'worship' meant going to church.

By the time I was a teenager, not only the clothes had changed. The Pentecostal movement had spread, and church services were half an hour longer to demonstrate our increased spirituality. Guitars replaced organs, overhead-projectors replaced the wooden hymn boards and all the singing was bunched together.

The word worship had a new definition. It was updated to mean emotionally charged congregational singing. Because the preaching was no longer interrupted with regular standing up and sitting down, pastors counteracted the tendency to fall asleep by shouting.

Time has elapsed. Women are wearing tiny glasses and ripped blue jeans. Meetings are two hours long and Pastor's roar. Electric guitars and drums have replaced the acoustic equivalents and power-point ousts the overhead projector. 'Worship' is a pop concert. We are encouraged to sing, however, joining in is difficult

Homemade Church

because the songs are not designed for congregational singing.

The new structure is as unyielding as the corset of the 1900s, all church services, seminars, and sometimes even working bees, start with an hour's 'worship' to call down God.

Jesus, by contrast, does not change or follow fashions. His definition of true worship is to look after the widows, and the orphans, and to keep one's self unpolluted from the world.

Perhaps we should drop the jargon and call singing, singing; and sing to the Lord from the heart when it seems appropriate.

Wendy Hamilton

The Second Child.

Acts 2:42
And they continued steadfastly in the apostle's doctrine and fellowship, and in the breaking of bread, and in prayers.

Every parent cuts their teeth on child number one. When child number two is expected they feel a little more confident. After all, they have been through this once before. It is a shock to find child two is a very different breed of bird.

Everything you did for number one does not work for number two and you are back to groping around in the dark again.

Andrew and Janine came to the second service of Chapel two, and quickly we recognized special chemistry between our two families. I had met Janine shortly before, at a ladies' camp. Unfortunately, I had

Homemade Church

a small accident on the way there. We had taken the Chapel sign down two months previously so the trucks could get the new building down the driveway. The night of the ladies' camp, I fell down the empty posthole while opening the gate in the dark. I was not hurt but one leg was covered in mud. I arrived at the camp with one blue jean leg, one brown jean leg, and a great story with which I entertained my friends.

That I was at a ladies' camp, was nothing short of a miracle. I do not like highly structured camps. What is more, this one had nine meetings squashed into two days. One of the nice things about reaching middle age is that I no longer feel compelled to stick to a program if it is overwhelming.

I picked out the bits that looked interesting and played truant for the rest. Consequently on Sunday morning (while the more sanctified ones were laboring through yet another meeting) I was doing chocolate cookies and coffee in my cabin. As I took my first bite, a tap, tap, tap, sounded on my door. I opened it and there stood Janine, coffee cup in hand.

"I heard you talking at the dinner table last night about a house-church you run," she said. "Could you tell me more?"

"Come in, come in, I love to tell a story," I said delighted.

Poor Janine, beginning, middle and end, she got the whole story. when I was finished, she knew all about Mount tiger Chapel and was keen to come to the next

Wendy Hamilton

service.

Despite my accident, by the time Chapel weekend rolled around again, the hole still gaped and the sign still reclined on the ground. Janine and Andrew searched the Mount Tiger road without finding us. Next Chapel Sunday, we replaced the sign in haste, sometime between putting out the chairs and buttering buns.

The Williams came, they searched, and this time they found us. It was the birth of a wonderful friendship and soon the birth of another kind. As Andrew and Janine saw what we were doing, the desire to run a house church arose in their hearts.

"We would like to have a go at this one day," said Andrew at lunch, taking a bite of raspberry bun.

Ian swallowed a sausage roll, "why not now?" he said.

"That's right," I chipped in, "we are nothing special; if we can do it, so can you."

"I'm not sure," said Janine hesitantly.

"If you want us to," said Ian, "we could come and help you until you don't need us anymore."

"That would be great," said Andrew lighting up.

So, Hukerenui Chapel was born on the second Sunday of the month in a tennis club hall. Because Hukerinui Chapel was our second child, we dressed him in Mount Tiger's clothes.

Janine sent a chatty newsletter around the immediate neighborhood and a hundred flyers around the wider area. We had a speaker ready to give his testimony,

Homemade Church

twenty plastic chairs ready for the farmer neighbors, and baking, buttered buns, and sausages ready for lunch. But Hukerenui Chapel did nothing.

I have learned that God's shut doors are as miraculous as his open ones, just not as fun. The day we got thrown out of the tennis club hall was the day Hukerenui Chapel woke up. Because we lost our building to the tennis season, Andrew and Ian built a modest shed for the meetings. It was similar to the chapel Dad and Ian built, but instead of sleeping cupboards, it had a large overhang for a carport. And instead of being a Chapel-cum-tractor-shed, it was a Chapel-cum-pottery-shop. Our first service was comfortably stuffed with families. And suddenly we saw Hukerenui's true breed. Not a collection of farmers, but a group of gentle home-schooling families. Not a cheeky Norton or Mum among them, (if you didn't count Emma or me).

Although the new shed was a step in the right direction, Hukerenui still wore borrowed clothes. The format right down to the plastic chairs and testimonies was Mount Tiger Chapel. The Tattersall's with eight children fixed that. They needed a place to stay, interim, while their house was built. They shifted into the shed, and Hukerenui Chapel shifted into Andrew and Janine's house.

The Williams living room was a great improvement. It was filled with comfortable overstuffed, 1930s chairs. Cats lounged on a big old couch, next to the overflowing bookcase and floral swaged curtains. Pottery jars of

Wendy Hamilton

roses stood on the honky-tonk piano and fish wafted through a castle in their glass tank. Yes, we still needed some of those plastic chairs, but no more rigid rows. We sat in a wobbly circle with bunches of kids sprawled over the carpet or on cushions. With so many mature Christians, we decided we did not need people to come and give their testimonies. Men spoke up one by one sharing from the Bible, what was on their heart.

Hukerenui finally had comfortable clothes that fit him and his own way of doing things. Sometimes we all bought along our instruments for a musical morning. As most of us were mediocre at best, nobody was embarrassed by a lack of ability.

Small children had shakers, clackers, and triangles; sometimes even pots and wooden spoons. Meanwhile, older kids and adults sported between them a trumpet, a pennywhistle, a couple of guitars, a flute, a bagpipe chanter, a squeezebox, a viola, and lots of violins. It was a motley sort of orchestra. Happily, the Bible says to make a joyful noise, not a lovely noise. And a joyful noise it certainly was.

Before and after the meeting we gathered in the kitchen that opened off the living room through double doors. In winter, we clustered by the antique wood range, our hands wrapped around steaming cups of coffee made with cream from Andrew's house cow.

As families arrived, the wooden countertop steadily filled with yummy things. After the meeting we sang 'Thank You Lord for Giving Us Food,' and filed

Homemade Church

around the table, laden with the former residents of the countertop and overflowing oven. Then, plates full, we drifted out onto the veranda or into the garden in ever-changing knots of three or four, for chatting and laughing and fellowship.

After lunch, kids were heard but seldom seen. The boys scattered over the ten acres in small bands of tree climbers, warriors, creek waders or hill sliders, while the girls rode the horse or mule, played with dolls houses or cooked potatoes on hobo stoves in an open field. During the summer on a particularly sultry afternoon, someone might suggest an impromptu swim. Then we all scrambled into a convoy of vans and headed off to a popular swimming hole a few miles down the road.

Just as a growing child needs new clothes from time to time, so Hukerenui developed, and therefore needed a change of clothes. Unfortunately, old ingrained traditions are hard to swim against, after a time, spontaneous sharing in the meetings dried up and uncomfortable silences ensued. The boredom barometers shuffled and scuffled; it was time for something different.

We came up with the idea that every family who was willing, would take the whole service for a morning. As each family had a strength peculiar to them, we decided to use Chapel mornings as practice sessions for potential summer outreaches. One family would present and the rest of us would cheer them on; and maybe in the summer, we would have enough confidence to have a go at a beach mission.

Wendy Hamilton

We had puppet shows, and flannel graphs, stories and chalk drawings, musical items, and quizzes. Most families had five-plus children and each child participated when it was their family's turn.

Then someone had the idea of Father-and-son camps; so occasionally, the men, with a horde of scuffling, shoving, excited, boys, hiked into the bush with tents and dried food for a weekend of roughing it.

Hukerenui became a vibrant established group within eighteen months. As a healthy child grows to the point, they are ready to fly on their own, Hukerenui didn't need Ian and my help anymore. We waved goodbye and went off to help give birth to a third house-church in Dargaville.

Homemade Church

Father and Son Weekends

Malachi 4:6
And he shall turn the heart of the fathers to the children, and the heart of the children to their fathers, lest I come and smite the earth with a curse.

Weekend camps for fathers and sons were very successful. The men and boys all enjoyed them and came home with family bonds strengthened. The shared experiences of sore backs, bugs, burned food, wood smoke clothes, and lack of baths, produced a special glue between them. I want to write about these camps, but as I am not a father or a son, I have never been to one. I was, however, at the daddy of a camp that begot the idea.

Wendy Hamilton

The next morning was Chapel Sunday

Homemade Church

We assembled one Friday evening at Mount Tiger, the Hamilton family, and the Williams family. Andrew (who is totally opposed to war) arrived clad in a bottle green army shirt and green army pants. He carried an army rifle while an army knife and bags of ammunition hung from his belt. Robbie and Edward were kitted out in a similar fashion, as closely as the Salvation Army thrift store could manage (an excellent place for family shopping.) Janine, Rebecca, Emily, and Suzy had on pretty floral dresses, while we Hamiltons were decked out in a motley assortment of jeans, shorts, and gumboots sourced from The Red Cross Shop (another excellent family store.).

We loaded the back of Ian's pickup with packs, chilly bins sleeping bags, rope and machetes. Then with Williams and Hamilton's squeezed into the cab, we slewed, skidded, bounced and jarred our way down the track to the bottom of the bush-clad valley. We stopped close to the wide pebbly stream and burst out of the front and side doors. Like Tibetan Sherpas, we hoisted luggage onto our backs preparatory to fording the stream and hiking up the other side of our Himalayas. Ian handed me a rifle and a weighty shoulder bag bursting with four hundred rounds of ammunition.

"Just how many goats and possums do you expect to shoot?" I said, my shoulder dropping under the weight.

"I don't know, it pays to be prepared."

I rolled my eyes in disbelief as I followed him up the hill.

Wendy Hamilton

The climb to the campsite was steep and slippery at parts, but we managed, even four-year-old Suzy. We had chosen the spot because it was one of the few flattish areas.

"Righto," said Andrew dumping his burden down. He picked up a machete and slashed at a nearby tall fern. "Come on, let's get to work."

Ian and the boys followed his example and set to work with gusto. Before long they had cleared a large enough patch. The idea was to live off the land as much as possible. Ian, however, disgraced our family by digging in the bottom of his pack for a bright blue plastic tarpaulin which he proceeded to rig up as a makeshift tent over some stout tree branches. It was cheating and soft. Marie, Hannah, Joe, and Mark hung their heads in shame. Their father with a plastic roof over his head instead of centipede infested *ponga fronds and ferns.

I experienced the uncomfortable sensation for the first time, of being unequally yoked in marriage. When I was a child, my family camped with a minimum of comfort. We camped during hurricanes in leaky tents with smoky lanterns and sand flies. Ian, on the other hand, had cruised about in a converted 1930s school bus, complete with bunk beds, sink bench, indoor camp cooker, and mosquito repellant. A sign-writer friend had painted the outside from windscreen to tow bar with Christian logos. Passing cars were treated to the sight of a mobile billboard trundling slowly down the motorway covered with, "Honk if you love Jesus,"

Homemade Church

"One Way Jesus," fish signs and "Jesus He's The Real thing," in a painted coca-cola shaped bottle.

"Aw come on, don't be such a town softy. You haven't experienced camping until you've slept under pongas[1] and pig fern," we all scoffed.

Despite group disapproval, Ian clung to his tarpaulin. I decided to forgo my pride and stand, "for better for worse" alongside my disgraced spouse and sleep under the blue plastic shame. The kids, however, redeemed some of the family respect by constructing sturdy-looking bivouacs.[2]

Now our accommodation was taken care of, it was time to set up the camp kitchen. Andrew and Ian hauled rocks up from the creek, stacked them in a ring and placed an old oven rack over the top to make a dandy fireplace. Then it was time for the unveiling of the food. The blue and red chilly bins were lugged close to the fireplace and we gathered around. The unveiling of our contribution was a non-event; merely a cooked chicken, a tin opener, and a stack of tins of Baked-Beans-in-Tomato-Sauce (an edible equivalent to the Swiss Army knife.)

Andrew's food selection was an entirely different matter. His choice electrified the group. Even Janine was taken-a-back as she had left the food organization to him. She had gone as far as to lift the coolers; enough

---

[1] Pongas are tall, tree ferns that grow in New Zealand
[2] Bivouacs are rough huts made from ferns, pongas and small trees.

to feel reassured by their weight. But she had not looked inside. The first lid revealed plastic drink bottles filled with clean drinking water, very boring. But what the second lid revealed when opened with a flourish was riveting. A decapitated, dead cat, freshly skinned and glowing muscle-red, glistened up at us. We all gawped at it in shocked silence.

"Beautiful rabbit, I shot this morning" enthused Andrew, "I thought we could boil it up for dinner with punga fronds and Palm tree.

"Ooo, that makes me feel sick," said Rebecca turning away hastily, "I thought it was our cat."

There were other similar comments from the rest of us. Andrew was mystified over our lack of enthusiasm over his menu. We ate the chicken I had planned for tomorrow's dinner by a vote of twelve to one and slumped into bed under the Southern Cross and the sparkling Milky Way.

The next morning almost everyone had slid out of their accommodation and down the hill a distance. That shiny fabric they make sleeping bags out of acts like molasses on a hot tin roof given the right conditions. We managed by careful strategies to avoid the rabbit all day. But by dinner time rations were getting low and there was no way of procrastinating any longer. I guess one of my chilly bins contained some potatoes because we had rabbit, potato, and ponga stew. Surprisingly (after our initial reluctance) we all had to agree it wasn't too bad. Moreover, nobody died because I made sure

Homemade Church

the kids collected only big ponga fronds for the cooking pot. They were pale green and covered with black fur like big hairy spider legs. I knew they were safe to eat unlike the small purple look-alike fronds because my sister nearly poisoned us when we were kids. You don't forget an experience like that. As we finished the last mouthful, our friend Andy-D. materialized out of the bush. His timing was superb. He had managed to avoid the rabbit stew (having dined on takeaways) and rode in like a knight in shining armor with a rescue supply of junk food. We built up the fire and sat around it in the deepening darkness, toasting marshmallows and feasting on nuts and chocolate bars. Andrew (who is totally opposed to war) regaled us with story after story of his exploits at the British Army training camp of his pre-Christian days.

"Then I threw some hand grenades, doubled back, shot up some flares, darted to the other side and shot a round of ammunition into the air. The whole group wound up sleeping in the car park, convinced a full army had attacked them. I didn't have much respect for their commander," he snorted. He picked up his rifle and shot a bullet at the moon. "Then another time," he said carrying on with his story, "I was in charge of an exercise, we had just laid out a string of spikes across the road when a huge combine harvester came over the hill and wrapped that line of spikes around his front wheels. The driver wasn't too happy. I took one look at those big tires hissing out air in three hundred and sixty-five directions and said, just charge it up to the British Army Sir,"

As I say, Andrew is totally opposed to war but there is something powerfully pleasant in smelly socks, army boots, hand grenades, and rifles.

A morepork interrupted Andrew with a sudden loud doleful MORE PORK! The noise came from above our heads, making us jump. Moreporks are a common night sound but you seldom hear them so close. But then seldom are you so far in the bush. Just then the deep throaty sound of a powerful stereo system rent the air.

"BOOM, BOOM, THUMMPY, THUMMPY, YAH, YAH, BOOM, BOOM, THUMMPY, THUMMPY, YAH, YAH."

Perhaps we weren't that far in the bush after all. Maybe we were in reality still on our own property. Blow that noisy Rider family for spoiling our illusion!

"Where's my cell phone? I'll ring up Noise Control and get them sorted out!" roared Ian.

"What! You've bought your cell phone?" I said appalled.

"Of course."

Further shame engulfed all Hamiltons at this new dreadful revelation. He could not get it to work, however; cell phone coverage is not reliable in the bottom of a valley. We spent the rest of the evening storytelling, singing and toasting marshmallows to the boisterous accompaniment of, "BOOM, BOOM, THUMMPY, THUMMPY, YAH, YAH!"

Homemade Church

The next morning was Chapel Sunday. We broke camp early, carted everything back to the pickup, and slipped, slewed, slid and juddered all the way back to the top. As we hastily cobbled together a play for the morning service, (still in our smoky clothes), Andrew remarked it had been a jolly good weekend.

"But next time," he said, "We should go down with only a tobacco tin survival kit each."

Janine and I gawped at him as if he was a skinned cat.

Since then Hukerenui has run several father and son Camps. Including a particularly memorable one, where Joe and Mark came home with Chickenpox. Lately, I have heard rumors that they are thinking of expanding to Father and Daughter Camps. As far as I know, nobody has tried the tobacco tin camp yet. I strongly suspect Andrew will encounter resistance to the idea from the daughters and Ian.

Wendy Hamilton

Boys and Legs.

Exodus 35:29
The children of Israel brought a willing offering unto the Lord, every man, and woman, whose heart made them willing to bring for all manner of work, which the Lord had commanded to be made by the hand of Moses.

We have always found joy in junk; other people's junk is treasure, our own junk is, well, just junk. So, the day that Ian got permission to demolish and keep some old shade houses, was cause for celebration. Full of jubilation, Ian phoned Andrew.

"Hey Andrew, I've been given a heap of shade-houses, do you want some.?"

"Too right," said Andrew enthusiastically.

"There are plenty for both of us and if we work together, it will make the job easier."

Homemade Church

"Yeah, and the boys could come too," said Andrew.

"Good thinking," said Ian, "they would be a big help."

Subsequently, on Saturday morning the two men, accompanied by their sons, met at the demolition site. After assigning the boys the simple job of sorting a pile of timber into short, middle-sized and long lengths, the men went happily away to pull off the roof. Two hours and one roof later, the men returned to find four pieces of lumber stacked and a full-scale sword fight in progress. The swords were carefully and lovingly made out of the shortest bits of the timber. A brave attempt at shaping the weapons with pocket knives left both boys and blades alike, looking somewhat scarred and gashed. Certainly, the gory element added to the authenticity of the battle scene.

"Why are there only four pieces of timber in the pile over there?" asked Ian his eyebrows jutting out in annoyance.

"I couldn't shift timber I got a prickle in my foot," said Robbie.

"I was too thirsty to work," said Joe.

"I needed to go to the bathroom," said Mark.

"Bending down and lifting makes me feel all faint," said Edward.

"I'm not impressed with your excuses," said Ian, "you have had two hours and done nothing."

"We are going to have a coffee break now and afterwards I expect you boys to get your back into moving lumber," said Andrew giving them all a hard look.

After a coffee, the men went off to remove all the rafters, leaving dire threats of docked pocket money if better progress was not made. At lunchtime, eight pieces of lumber lay sorted into short, mid and long lengths, and a vigorous game was in full swing.

"What are you doing," said Andrew grabbing a rock off Robbie.

"We're playing marbles," said Joe.

"You are supposed to be stacking timber," growled Ian. "Mr. Williams and I have demolished six shade houses in the time you have moved these," he pointed at the pitiful pile.

"I couldn't lift anything," said Robbie, "my arms got spasms in them."

"My legs came over all funny," said Joe.

"I needed to got to the bathroom again," said Mark.

"I can feel a head ache coming on," said Edward.

"You don't need two hours to go to the bathroom and there is nothing wrong with arms that can throw marbles," said Andrew, pointing at the pile of rocks scattered about.

"That's right," said Ian. "Joe and Mark I'm fining you fifty cents."

"That goes for you too, Edward and Robbie," said Andrew sitting on the lumber. "Go and get the cooler from the van and we will have lunch."

After sandwiches and tea, the men stood up.

Homemade Church

"Now boys, when we come back this next time, we want to see a big pile of neatly stacked lumber," said Andrew.

"None of this mucking around," said Ian, as he and Andrew went off to dismantle walls.

At afternoon tea time, the men came back to find twelve sticks of stacked timber, a large ring of heavy rocks and water boiling merrily in an old can on a well-fed fire. Edward meanwhile, had a terrible case of potential sunburn, Joe had lost his shoes, Robbie thought he had sunstroke, and Mark (who is a boy apt to overdo a good idea) needed another three hours in the bathroom. After a hearty afternoon tea for two, (the saying if a man will not work, he will not eat, applies equally to boys), the men once more set off and once more returned. This time the pile had grown to twenty-four pieces of sorted timber.

"What are you doing?" roared Ian goaded into anger.

"We are blowing up ants," said Joe holding up his magnifying glass.

"It's a good education," said Robbie justifying their actions.

"That's it," said Andrew, "no dinner until all the lumber is stacked and loaded onto the trailer.

"What?" they said appalled.

"And we will sit here and watch you," added Ian.

"How mean can fathers get," grumbled Edward picking up a small stick. "Making us work like slaves when we are sick and have worked hard all day!"

Wendy Hamilton

At Mount tiger Chapel there was only one rule; no one was allowed to do anything they didn't want to. (children excepted). None of this SUPPORTING THE PROGRAM stuff. If the program was so weak it needed supporting, let it die. All of us who had experienced a previous church life had also experienced at some time, a Pastor who had received a VISION and lashed us from the pulpit with word-whips barbed with thorny guilt. His aim was to motivate us to work. His method was less than 20% successful at motivating us. But as to inducing guilt, his success rate shot up to a staggering 100%. Sure, we all wanted to see people saved and the church grow, but some of the corporate methods the LEADER was commanding us to get involved with, stirred our hearts as much as sorting timber interests boys.

"Only do what overflows from your heart," was our motto. So, there was no Sunday school (none of us wanted to teach or attend it,) there was no evangelism committee, no nursery, no board meetings, and no treasurer, (we did not take money so there was no need for one) no kitchen roster, no working bees and no music practices.

We did, however, have erratic bulletins when the Spirit-led, and Mum in a sudden burst of inspiration got scribbling and posted a chatty heartfelt one in all the neighbor's letter-boxes. The CHAPEL CHATTER was full of jokes, pithy sayings, and funny, yet poignant, testimonies of Mum's walk with the Lord. It certainly

Homemade Church

wasn't your normal church bulletin. Even the roughest heathens loved them and were disappointed when they eventually stopped.

We also had impromptu testimonies, and prayer sessions, original poems, drawings, cards, and letters of encouragement circulating regularly. Marie our budding florist, always had a bunch of flowers made up in readiness for someone in need of a little cheering up that morning. Home-made apple and rhubarb pies, muffins, asparagus rolls and all sorts of goodies appeared each month. How they got from the kitchen to the lunch table so beautifully, I'll never know as I was always too busy in the back room talking and listening to someone who had caught my eye as hurting.

The women exchanged books, and teaching tapes, hand-me-down clothes, toys, and child-rearing tips, over lunch. While the men swapped stories and advice on work situations over the B.B.Q and organized a day to fix Chrystal's leaky roof and a date for the next Father and Son Camp.

As for those four boys who could only sort one stick of timber every two hours, they were outside manhandling hundreds of demolition bricks; stacking them into forts for mock battles. Somehow with everything else going on, none of us missed Sunday school, committees, working bees or music practices.

There is a very steep and high hill behind Andrew's house. At the top is a heavy wooden pallet. It sits there as a permanent monument which Andrew points out

Wendy Hamilton

to all his friends. In a burst of enthusiasm for a game, Robbie and Edward huffed and puffed and dragged it up there with strength and ease. But after the game finished, a curious weakening of the legs and arm muscles prevented any return of it to its proper position. It is amazing what hard work boys can do if they truly want too. It is also amazing what God's adult children can do when they are left to do only what overflows from the heart.

Homemade Church

Mary.

Hebrews 5:12
For when for the time ye ought to be teachers, ye have need that one teach you again which be the first principles of the oracles of God; and are become such as have need of milk and not of strong meat.

Our four Grandparents lived six hundred miles away. When Antoinette was five years old, she took it upon herself to rectify this shortcoming and went relative hunting. Six doors down the hill she struck cake in an elderly woman and her spinster daughter; Mrs. Martin and Mary.

Mrs. Martin and Mary were fascinatingly fat. They had got that way through the delicate art of sumptuous afternoon teas. Their wide girth made it necessary to navigate doorways with a diagonal sideways shuffle;

Wendy Hamilton

especially if they were carrying a tea tray loaded with the fruit of their hands, cream puffs, chocolate eclairs, melting moments, truffles, tarts, the list goes on and on. Because hips do not cope too well with carrying the weight of three people full time, the cream puffs and melting moments rocked from side to side gently as Mrs. Martin (clutching the tea tray) undulated across the carpet with an eccentric wheel motion. Once she had gained the safe harbor of the circle of armchairs, the three-tiered plates of dainty fatties were transferred to a waiting afternoon tea table where the floral china tea cups and milk jug were already assembled. The tea, encased in its pompom-topped, knitted tea cozy, was nicely brewed. Antoinette, Rubella, and I sitting like turkeys on a rail, waited with excited anticipation.

Mary was an only child and had never married. She and her mother were both old enough, by the time Antoinette went relative hunting, to be grandmas and were as delighted to find new relatives as we were. Their primary language of love was food and this was certainly a language we kids related to and appreciated. Left to our own inclinations we would have appreciated it on a larger scale, unfortunately, we had strict instructions from Mum.

"Only two servings each," she said before we left home.

Naturally, we took much time choosing our cakes, and always passed over the club sandwiches. We were not going to waste this moment on sandwiches, even

Homemade Church

cream cheese and ham ones. Much thought also went into the choice of the china plate our two dainties temporarily sat upon. There was a large stack in the china cabinet with rounded corners.

"Should I have the red rosebud one or the purple pansy one with the gold outline?" I wondered each visit.

The cat was never forgotten. He always had his afternoon-tea-saucer-of-milk. He was a ginger neutered Tom-cat with a mild nature and a body to match his mistresses. We could hardly pick him up he was so huge and heavy.

He always had breakfast, morning tea, lunch, afternoon tea, dinner, and supper. He too undulated slowly over the carpet on eccentric wheel hips. He had one extra fascination. A certain spot on his back activated frenzied chewing on his left front leg when scratched. The neighbors knew when we had recently been for a visit, as Jasper's left leg would have a little shining bald patch.

Sometimes for a special treat, we stayed the night in the big bed in the spare room. Breakfast was served with the same nicety as afternoon tea. The china teacups, rosebud plates, and pom-pom topped teapot were all there. But instead of in the lounge by the armchairs, they were on the oak dining table with fluted legs. And instead of cream puffs and eclairs, there were pancakes with sugar and cream and a nice soft-boiled egg in a china egg cup. Really, choosing your own relatives has a lot going for it.

Wendy Hamilton

The cat chewed his leg when we scratched his back

Homemade Church

As a ten-year-old I did not see past the cakes, apple lined laundry, loaded grapevine, and the cat's leg. I loved going there and I loved Mrs. Martin and Mary. But as time went by and I matured, I started to notice things beyond cream puffs.

Mrs. Martin was possessive of Mary, and Mary had never grown beyond age sixteen. Her age in calendar years might be 66, 67, 68, but in reality, every year she turned sixteen. She had never pushed past the teenage hurdles into life. Whenever a difficulty presented itself, Mary took to bed and cried for a day, a week, or a month, until the nasty thing disappeared.

When her mother died, we all worried about Mary and wondered how she would cope. But for a time, all was well. Despite the grief of losing her mother, she was on a high and pushed forward in new strides, selling the old house and purchasing an almost identical one a few streets down the road.

She hired a gardener a couple of hours a week and the garden lit up with bright marigold and petunias. Ian and I visited her often. Every visit (after we had admired the changes the painters were making to the house) we enjoyed a luscious dinner and a sumptuous dessert. Sometimes Ian would drive her 1920s Holden car and the three of us meandered out to the country for an afternoon picnic.

But other times when we visited, Mary would be DOWN. The house was dirty, unwashed dishes stacking up in the kitchen and unwashed Mary in bed, crying and reading romance novels. This could go on for eight months at a stretch. We learned to gauge Mary's moods by her bedroom curtains. As we zoomed into her driveway on our little 125cc motorbike, we quickly scanned the left-hand windows, "good," they were open; she was up. "Oh no," they were closed; she was still DOWN.

Without her mother to carry life along while she was in bed, things deteriorated quickly. Mary's overly conscientious cousin stepped into the breach and washed and cooked and enabled Mary to slip back to sixteen again. I learned through Mary that aging is mandatory but maturing is optional. Her gravestone says she died at age seventy-two, but in reality, she was sixteen.

Spiritual maturity is also optional. From time to time we had people come along to Mount Tiger and really love it. They loved the freedom and loved the atmosphere. They were unhappy and unfulfilled in their own church but after a while they left and went back. Their church was not meeting their needs any better, rather, it always boiled down to authority. There is something comforting in having a spiritual father figure between ourselves and God.

Just as pushing through to be a fully functioning adult requires taking risks and responsibilities for your own life, so too, discarding a pastor and going directly to Jesus for direction can be scary. It is not enough to listen to someone else's opinion. We must be searching the Bible; praying and seeking God's will ourselves.

Homemade Church

The buck of my mistakes stays with me.

House churches without authority figures are not for everyone. Not everyone wants to mature and leave home.

Wendy Hamilton

Shoemaker Discipleship

Acts 4:13
Now when they saw the boldness of Peter and John and perceived they were unlearned and ignorant men, they marveled; and they took knowledge of them, that they had been with Jesus.

How many remember the saying, "An ounce of theory is worth a pound of practice?"

I used to hear it a lot when I was a child, but I doubt any children nowadays have heard of it, as educational fashions have swung in favor of theoretical rather than practical learning. When I was young, it was different; apprenticeships were still around in abundance. A hundred years ago, that's how all trades were passed on. A boy of twelve was apprenticed to a shoemaker to

Homemade Church

learn the trade of shoemaking. As he was pretty useless and more of a nuisance than he was worth at first, the boy's family paid the shoemaker a fee to compensate the Master for his effort. The boy worked with his master during the day doing simple jobs, to begin with, like sweeping the floor. Eventually, he would get more capable and be given harder jobs until he was a skilled shoemaker himself. Apprenticeships in those days, were like discipleship because the boy also lived with his master as one of the family.

Christianity is more like a trade than a profession and passed on better by an apprenticeship than lectures. Just as a shoemaker who knows the history of shoes, but can't make a shoe is useless, a Christian who cannot translate bible knowledge into practical living is useless.

When a baby bird is little, the mother does not dump a big wriggling worm in front of her babies and expect them to eat it. First, she chews it up and then regurgitates it already digested for her babies. Formal bible studies are big worms. A baby Christian needs to be fed digested food. When Chrystal became born again, the standard Bible study did not work. She needed one on one customized regurgitation. Instead of a ladies' bible study, she visited or called those of us who had known the Lord a long time.

"Wendy what do I do about my horrible neighbor?" she asked me one day. "I hate him; this love your enemy bit is hard to swallow."

"I know, that's a tough one and I don't have all the

answers," I said, "but I will tell you a true story. When we first shifted into our house in town, my neighbor hated me for no reason. She would only speak to me to complain. I found myself hating her back, nasty thoughts were uppermost in my mind all the time."

"Yeah," said Chrystal, "that is exactly how I feel."

"I didn't want to even try to love her. Nevertheless, I gritted my teeth and started praying God would bless, help and save her. It was hard work."

"I bet," said Chrystal. "At first, I often thought nasty things for an hour or more until I remembered to pray. But as time went on, I prayed quicker and found it easier to do. Little by little my attitude changed and I started to see her as a broken, threatened woman rather than an ogre. Eventually, my children made friends with her over the fence and bit by bit the walls between us came down. I found out later she had been harassed by the neighbor on the other side of me. I was a similar age to that neighbor and she was afraid I was the same. She turned out to be the best neighbor I have ever had. She became Grandma to my children and spoiled us all."

"Hmm," said Chrystal thoughtfully, "it won't be easy praying for my neighbor, but I will give it a go."

Just as a mother bird presents the worm in a way the baby can digest, true discipleship means spending our time and sharing our innermost-being with another in the areas they are grappling with.

Jesus taught his disciples like a shoemaker, not a college professor.

Homemade Church

The End of the Picnic.

John 12:24
Verily, verily, I say unto you, Except a corn of wheat fall unto the ground and die, it abideth alone: but if it die it bringeth forth much fruit.

I am inclined to think God views churches as temporary paper cups or tents, while we definitely equate them with Egyptian pyramids, enduring until the world's end. We have all seen them, dead churches, empty save a few ultra-tough water-bugs; six old ladies faithfully attending a camping picnic that finished years ago; petrified paper cups used and re-used by a few, instead of thrown away after the party moved on.

Wendy Hamilton

The last Chapel service

Homemade Church

Our prayer for Mount Tiger Chapel right from the start was, "Lord, don't let us go a day longer than you want us to."

On Chapel-Saturdays, Mum added, "Please Lord could this be the last time." (Mum hated Chapel-Saturday more than any of us.) On Sunday evening she amended it to, "Thank you Lord that it wasn't the last time, that was wonderful."

I have always identified with the Israelites in the desert, how they followed the cloud. When the cloud lifted, they packed up their tents, when the cloud moved, they moved with it, when the cloud settled, they pitched their tents and settled. For twenty-three years the cloud was settled for Ian and me. Then one day it gently fluttered and lifted. Our settled life wobbled slightly with rumors of redundancies.

"I don't think there is much to worry about," said Ian. "My job is pretty secure. They are not getting rid of the technical staff."

"Yeah," I nodded, "I'm not concerned."

But as the cloud lifted higher, it dawned on us things were afoot spiritually.

"We have been settled for twenty-three-years," I said to Ian one night. "That is a long time. If God wants us to move on, he will remove your job."

Oddly, it was a promotion, not redundancy that catapulted us out. A strange sort of promotion, up from middle management to senior management, loads more responsibility, lots more liability and not so much as a can of mackerel in extra remuneration. Nobody had heard of such a thing. I have learned to look for God's fingerprints when something strange happens.

"You can't stay," I said to Ian, "it is going to irk you that the guys under you with less responsibility are paid more than you."

"What shall I do?" said Ian.

"God must have something up his sleeve," I said, "we had a feeling this might happen."

"I could do a Ph.D. if I can't get a job," said Ian. "We have often thought about doing that."

"Hmm. Do you think Professor Sammes was serious all those times he has invited you to America to do a Ph.D. there?" I asked, considering the possibility as serious for the first time. "I always thought he was joking."

"That's a thought," said Ian his eyes sparkling. "I was thinking of doing one here in New Zealand; America would be an adventure."

"Phone him and see if he was serious," I said.

One call and suddenly it was as if a mighty vacuum cleaner was turned onto full blast and sucking us to the USA. We set the date for the last Chapel service on the first Sunday of December 2006. Everyone was sad. There was talk of petrifying the paper cup.

"Perhaps, Anne and Harold you could continue running the chapel after Ian and Wendy leave," said Norton, looking at Mum and Dad hopefully.

"We are too old," said Dad.

Homemade Church

"Besides, we need to rent out the property to help us survive financially," said Ian.

The biggest reason of all, however, was the still small voice in our hearts.

"Unless a grain of wheat, fall to the ground and die, it abides alone," it whispered. "Lord, help us not to go a day beyond your purpose," we answered.

Sixty was about the maximum amount of people we could stuff into the chapel. Every Chapel-Saturday we prayed, "Lord not too many, only let those who are meant to be here, come."

God was gracious and we always got everyone inside, but often it was a cozy squeeze. The little building on the last day was packed to bursting. That morning, the lesson was on Moses and the ten plagues rather than the more traditional nativity scenes you would expect to see in early December. There was great hilarity as confetti, rubber insects, rice and chocolate ladybird plagues, flew through the air and fell among us, as Moses confronted Pharaoh, and Pharaoh (resplendent in a bathrobe topped with a towel and plastic snake headdress) resisted.

Right to the end, Mount Tiger Chapel was uniquely Mount Tiger Chapel. Not once was the last service retrospective, it looked forward and encouraged us all onward. As the final kiss of blessing, two more neighbors gave their hearts to the Lord that morning, and our beloved Norton who has become a strong man of God, opened up his home for a weekly bible study to disciple them.

Wendy Hamilton

We waved the last car goodbye

Homemade Church

Then our dear neighbors (now fellow Christians) gathered around us and sent us out from among them with prayer.

When the last car disappeared down the long driveway, it occurred to me we had run the Chapel for exactly seven years. Wow! Our prayers had been answered. We had not gone on a day longer than we should have.

Wendy Hamilton

About the Author

Wendy and her husband Ian ran house churches in New Zealand from the year 2000 to 2007.
In 2007and 2008, Wendy and Ian were involved in house-churches in Connecticut and Colorado.

Homemade Church grew out of interaction with the Colorado folk who struggled with the transition to organic church more than the Christians of Connecticut and New Zealand. Some of the most frustrated people were ex-pastors, who had left their livelihoods out of a deep conviction that there was a better and more biblical way to do church. These brave men felt their formal training and other people's expectations were getting in the way of developing something new. Something needed to be written to move mid-western churches beyond the little mini-versions of the institutional church model.

Homemade Church

Wendy and Ian are fifth-generation conservative Christians. Both Wendy and Ian taught Sunday School and Ian held positions as Church Treasurer and Deacon. After years of discontentment, they and their four children took the scary step of leaving the established church. Wendy's desire is this book will bring hope and validation to the many invisible Christians in the church who yearn for a more authentic way of gathering together with fellow believers.

Wendy Hamilton

Other Books By Wendy Hamilton

Eating a Light Bulb does not make you Bright
Light on Home-schooling

Darling the Window is on Fire

I told you not to Climb the Cactus.
Surviving the Badlands of Motherhood

Children's Novels
The Britwhistles win a Prize
The Britwhistles and the Elasticizer

Children's Picture books
The Unlucky Snails
The Unlucky Snails go to France

These can be found at
www.zealauspublishing.com

www.ingramcontent.com/pod-product-compliance
Lightning Source LLC
Chambersburg PA
CBHW021111080526
44587CB00010B/478